JAN -- 2023

D0847044

... of a cookbook! In a busy world filled with stress after stress, it is ... make something quick and delightful!"

—molly bernard, actress ...

"If you want to start out with a nutritious breakfast and end up with a complete and delicious dinner READ THIS BOOK!"

—faye kellerman, *NYT* bestselling crime author

"Food fast now! This book is it!"

—margaret cho, stand-up comedian and actress

"I cannot run a six-minute mile, but I can cook a six-minute meal. Because of Karen, I am able to call myself a cooker. Anyone can handle six minutes."

—alex borstein, actress and comedian

"This cookbook checks all my boxes: easy to make, delicious and time to spare."

—kelly rutherford, actress and founder of Sovereign Collective

"These are fun and different recipes for the chef in all of us."

—heather mcdonald, host of the Juicy Scoop with Heather McDonald podcast

"Karen makes cooking and eating well easy, cost effective, delicious, nourishing and fun."

—tara stiles, co-founder of Strala Yoga

"I am so inspired by Karen and her delicious and easy recipes. I believe cooking can be fun, healthy, easy and tasty and that's exactly what Karen has provided for all of us."

—paolo presta, host of A Spoonful of Paolo

"There's not much to say except that all our lives are filled with chaos and Karen's recipes supports us in a way that we can thrive."

—zara terez tisch, founder & CEO of Terez

"Karen's recipes are easy, accessible and delicious."

—joey slotnick, film and voice actor

"I love a full house of friends and family, but what I DON'T love is hours of tolling in the kitchen—that's why these recipes are so awesome; they only use a few ingredients and are super easy to make if you're not Martha Stewart."

—jill kargman, author, writer and actress

"Karen just really gets it. She knows moms need recipes that are quick and easy and she delivers on every page!"

—laurie gelman, author and television personality

"Karen gets what it's like to be busy, but I love that she's helping people to NOT abandon family dinners amid the chaos."

—wendi mclendon-covey, actor, writer, producer

"I love that Karen provides simple and delicious recipes. Her down-to-earth personality and relatable humor will keep you coming back for more!"

—jamie greenberg, celebrity makeup artist

"Karen gets that I'm a busy dad with hungry kids. She also understands the best way to enjoy the Chicago Bears game is with a plate of her sriracha honey wings. I'm gearing up for next season, armed with these recipes, ready to feed my houseful of hungry fans."

—gabe ramirez, radio host 670 The Score and B96

DEDICATION

To my readers—May your hearts and tables be full,
and to my husband and boys who forever fill mine.

PAGE STREET
PUBLISHING CO.

Copyright © 2022 Karen Nochimowski

First published in 2022 by
Page Street Publishing Co.
27 Congress Street, Suite 1511
Salem, MA 01970
www.pagestreetpublishing.com

All rights reserved. No part of this book may be reproduced or used, in any form or by any means, electronic or mechanical, without prior permission in writing from the publisher.

Distributed by Macmillan, sales in Canada by The Canadian Manda Group.

26   25   24   23   22   1   2   3   4   5

ISBN-13: 978-1-64567-661-4
ISBN-10: 1-64567-661-7

Library of Congress Control Number: 2022938236

Cover and book design by Katie Beasley for Page Street Publishing Co.
Photography by Toni Zernik

Printed and bound in the United States

Page Street Publishing protects our planet by donating to nonprofits like The Trustees, which focuses on local land conservation.

6-minute dinners and more!

100 super simple dishes

with 6 Minutes of Prep and 6 Ingredients or Less

karen nochimowski

creator of
m🌸mmachef

PAGE STREET
PUBLISHING CO.

Glenview Public Library
1930 GLENVIEW ROAD
GLENVIEW, ILLINOIS 60025
847-729-7500

TABLE OF CONTENTS

INTRODUCTION

Many of us grew up dreaming of having people gathered around our dinner table, enjoying a great meal and sharing stories about our days. Dreams don't instantly become reality. In fact, our dreams can quickly evaporate when work schedules, appointments, kids and screen distractions enter the picture. Tasks such as making dinner can seem overwhelming. Yet, I believe the simple joy and comfort of coming together for meals is needed now more than ever.

My name is Karen, and I'm here to help make your daily dinner dreams a reality.

I've always found sanctuary in the kitchen, and cooking has been a lifelong love. When I was younger, I had loads of time to create dinner party menus and could easily spend hours in the kitchen preparing elaborate meals. However, those leisurely days were replaced with a full and busy family life: three rambunctious boys, a hungry husband and a playful dog. Despite this seismic shift, my love of cooking and its power to bring people together remained steady. The problem was how to *make it work*.

With one kid on my hip, another playing on the floor and the third needing a ride to soccer practice, I could easily have relied on boxed meals and fast food. But instead of becoming a frequent flyer of the frozen pizza aisle at the grocery store, I forced myself to reinvent and reshape meals to meet the nutritional needs of picky palates, all within my limited time frame. It wasn't always easy. It took time—and lots of trial and error—but eventually, I became the queen of preparing delicious meals with a short prep time and just a handful of ingredients.

Friends and family kept asking for my culinary secrets, and I was thrilled to share. I started the Momma Chef blog to help people like me serve fabulous meals easily. After quickly garnering tens of thousands of viewers on my blog, I found a community who desperately needed what I was offering.

If you lack the luxury of time, you've picked up the right book—*6-Minute Dinners (and More!)* has you covered. Here, you'll find more than 100 recipes for healthy, satisfying dishes that will help put meals on your table. It's perfect for busy people who want to cook but who find that life keeps getting in the way. Every recipe uses no more than six ingredients with no more than six minutes of prep time. To be clear, cooking time does not equal prep time. "Cooking time" means you can walk away and deal with life outside the kitchen. "Prep time" means the minutes you are needed on task. And most of us—hopefully!—can dedicate six minutes to meal prep.

Consider this "six under six" cookbook your playbook for kitchen success, with me as your motivating team captain. In this playbook, you'll be equipped with my tried-and-true recipes. Many are traditional family favorites that I've tweaked for time and ease of preparation. Others are personal creations, inspired by our family trips, a craving or simply by what I had in my refrigerator on a given night. I'm blessed to live with four opinionated taste-testers, and they've all given these dishes their stamps of approval. You're going to love what's in store for you—familiar favorites as well as exciting new flavors and foods to serve to your own home team. I'm so excited for us to get started! I'll be here coaching you on every page and cheering for you every step of the way.

Welcome to the team. I'm so glad you're here!

XOXO,
Karen

Dietary Notes

The exponential increase of allergies and food sensitivities among children has changed the way I think about cooking. I've seen the struggles of my friends and readers trying to find a meal that is "safe" for everyone around the table.

In this cookbook, you will find clear labeling and indexing for recipes that are, or can be made, dairy free, egg free, gluten free, low carb, nut free, sesame free and vegetarian.

HERE ARE THE DIETARY CODES THAT CAN BE FOUND IN THE BOOK:

DF: Dairy Free

EF: Egg Free

GF: Gluten Free

LC: Low Carb

NF: Nut Free

SF: Sesame Free

V: Vegetarian

*Gluten can be found in dressings, sauces, stocks, gravies, marinades, condiments and other prepackaged ingredients; please be sure to always check the label when preparing something gluten free to make sure it is labeled as such or does not contain any gluten ingredients.

THE MAIN EVENT

I'm a fan of cookbooks. They've helped me plan menus, honed my kitchen techniques and deepened my culinary knowledge. I love the photos, and I love the stories. However, where most cookbooks fall short is the false promise that "once I make this recipe, dinner is served." Ha! That's some top-notch magical thinking. We all know there's more to getting dinner on the table than simply making a recipe: There's grocery shopping, meal preparation and cleanup. There are picky eaters to please and schedules to accommodate.

Our best-laid plans of providing daily home-cooked meals can easily be derailed by our busy lives. Who hasn't succumbed to ordering a pizza or picking up fast food over preparing dinner at home? But that's not what I wanted for my family—and if you're here, I know that's not what you want for your family either.

That's why this cookbook opens with a focus on dinner. Here, you'll find favorite dinner recipes that I've collected through the years and then streamlined to minimize preparation. Others were inspired by a trip, an ingredient or a craving—and always with a focus on ease, taste and time. With only 6 minutes of prep time and no more than six ingredients, this treasure trove of recipes will equip you to make dinner without sacrificing hours of prep and cleanup. Truly, the most time-consuming task in this chapter is answering the universal question of most wedding RSVPs: *chicken or beef?*

If you're leaning toward beef, start with the Smoked Barbecue Brisket Sliders on page 27— hands down a crowd-pleaser. You can also warm up your family on a cold winter night with the Perfect Beef Pot Roast on page 11. For a special holiday meal or company dinner, try the delicious and beautifully presented Braised Lamb Shanks with Pomegranate Glaze on page 16.

If you're more in the mood for chicken, start with this: Honey-Curry Chicken on page 39. (Truly. I know that we *just* met, but I would not lie to you. Promise me you'll check it out!) You'll find the Country "Fried" Chicken on page 31 so mouthwateringly delicious, you won't believe how simple it is. The festive Sheet-Pan Chicken Fajitas on page 40 provide the perfect shortcut to getting dinner on the table.

It's time to gather your six ingredients and get your dinner on!

PERFECT BEEF POT ROAST

(DF, EF, GF, LC, NF, SF)

You know that you've seriously entered adulthood when you make pot roast for the first time. If you've been waiting for the perfect recipe to take the plunge, I've got you covered. Just remember that although the dish can be prepped in minutes, it takes several hours to cook. However, it's those magical hours that add to its appeal. The heavenly aroma drifts from room to room, building anticipation for a shared family meal.

The slow-cooking process creates the ideal conditions for cooking root vegetables alongside the roast. Here, we stick with carrots, as I like to serve the roast with a side of mashed potatoes or buttered noodles. However, you can just as easily add potatoes, pearl onions or parsnips.

Prep Time: 5 minutes   Cook Time: 3 to 4 hours   Serves 6

Preheat the oven to 275°F (135°C).

In a large pot or Dutch oven, heat the oil over medium-high heat. Sear the top and bottom of the roast for about 2 minutes per side.

Add the carrots and beef broth to the pot.

Sprinkle the onion soup mix over the top of the roast, and add the rosemary.

Cover the pot, and place it in the oven to cook for 3 to 4 hours until the meat is tender, checking occasionally to make sure there is still liquid in the pot. If needed, add ½ cup (120 ml) of water at a time.

Alternatively, you can make this in the slow cooker: Add all the ingredients to the slow cooker, and cook on low for 6 to 8 hours or high for 3 to 4 hours until the meat is very tender.

Season with salt to your liking.

2 tablespoons (30 ml) extra-virgin olive oil

1 (3- to 4-pound [1.4- to 1.8-kg]) boneless beef chuck roast

8 unpeeled whole carrots, quartered

3 cups (720 ml) beef broth

1 (1-ounce [27-g]) envelope onion soup mix (my favorite is Lipton® Onion Soup Mix)

3 sprigs fresh rosemary

Salt, to taste

BEEF KEBABS ON CINNAMON STICKS

(DF, EF, GF, LC, SF)

Here's an inviting and flavorful way to serve ground beef without a bun. A perfect paleo delight! In this case, the skewers are flavorful cinnamon sticks. But, hey—the skewers are for flavor, not for eating. While the kebabs are cooking, the cinnamon sticks add a delectable earthy flavor to the meat.

I like to serve this dish with hummus. And guess what? Making homemade hummus is super easy, too! It's such a quick process that you can put it together while the kebabs are on the grill. Momma Chef is all about efficiency. All you need is a blender, 5 minutes and six ingredients to make Easy-Peasy Hummus (see page 102).

Prep Time: 5 minutes   Cook Time: 10 minutes   Makes 15 kebabs

In a large mixing bowl, combine the ground beef, allspice, seasoning salt, parsley and pine nuts.

Mix until everything is well combined.

Divide the meat into about 15 golf ball–sized balls, and push a cinnamon stick through the middle of each ball. Shape the meat around the cinnamon stick to form a football shape.

Preheat the grill to low heat, and grill the kebabs for 3 to 5 minutes per side, or until the preferred level of doneness.

You can also pan-fry these: Heat 2 tablespoons (30 ml) of olive oil in a large frying pan, and cook the kebabs for about 5 minutes per side until they are cooked through.

> **TIP:** If you are serving these to someone with nut allergies, you can skip the pine nuts.

1½ pounds (680 g) ground beef (at least 90 percent lean)

½ teaspoon allspice

1 teaspoon seasoning salt

½ cup (30 g) chopped fresh parsley

¼ cup (34 g) pine nuts (see Tip)

15 cinnamon sticks

THE BEST HOMEMADE SLOPPY JOES

(DF, EF, GF, NF, SF)

One fine day, my son told me that he was ready to join the sloppy joe fan club. Had I been physically able to do a backflip, you better believe I would have flipped for joy across my kitchen floor. Sloppy joes are super easy to make, and they are true crowd-pleasers. I immediately added them to the weekly menu rotation.

Fun fact: Pseudonyms abound for the loose-meat sandwich. In Nebraska, it's called a "yum yum," and in Rhode Island, "dynamite." A school menu in North Dakota names it a "slushburger," and in parts of Maryland, you'd order up a "steamer." Challenge your diners to create their own name, but as Shakespeare might say, "A sloppy joe by any other name would taste just as delicious"—especially if you use my favorite recipe!

Prep Time: 5 minutes   Cook Time: 10 minutes   Serves 4

In a large skillet, heat the oil over medium heat, and cook the ground beef, using a wooden spoon to break up the meat, until browned, about 5 minutes.

Drain any excess fat (if needed), and return the beef to the pan.

Stir in the ketchup, vinegar and brown sugar, and cook over medium heat for 5 minutes.

Serve on the hamburger buns.

1 tablespoon (15 ml) cooking oil of choice

1 pound (454 g) ground beef (see Tip)

½ cup (120 ml) ketchup

2 teaspoons (10 ml) apple cider vinegar

2 tablespoons (28 g) light brown sugar

4 hamburger buns, split (if making gluten free, get gluten-free buns)

TIP: You can use ground turkey in place of ground beef. By the way, these are called "sloppy janes." No joke!

BRAISED LAMB SHANKS WITH POMEGRANATE GLAZE

(DF, EF, GF, NF, SF)

Our family, like most, has tried-and-true holiday traditions that we follow and cherish each year. Not surprisingly, many of my family's holiday rituals center on food. I love the personal culinary challenge of presenting a new dish to see if it has what it takes to "make the team" of our beloved holiday menus. In 2020, I perfected an ideal dish for Christmas, Easter and Passover: braised lamb shanks. The pomegranate juice adds a bit of sweetness that brings out the delectable flavor of the lamb. And with this beautiful presentation, no one will believe that it took just 5 minutes to prep. Your family and holiday guests will definitely be impressed with this easy and delicious recipe. It's destined to be the star of your holiday dinner table.

Prep Time: 5 minutes   Cook Time: 3 hours   Serves 4

In a gallon-sized zip-top bag, mix the pomegranate juice, honey, rosemary, salt and garlic. Add the lamb shanks to the bag, and, if possible, let them marinate for at least 2 hours in the refrigerator.

Preheat the oven to 300°F (149°C).

In a Dutch oven, place the lamb shanks with their marinade, and add ½ cup (120 ml) of water.

Cover the pot, and bake for 3 hours.

You can also make this in a slow cooker: Place the lamb shanks with their marinade in a slow cooker, and add in ½ cup (120 ml) of water. Cover, and cook on low for 6 hours or on high for 3 hours.

2 cups (480 ml) pomegranate juice

¼ cup (60 ml) honey

1 tablespoon (2 g) chopped fresh rosemary

1 teaspoon kosher salt

3 cloves garlic, chopped

3 lamb shanks (about 4 pounds [1.8 kg])

OLD-FASHIONED BRAISED BRISKET

(DF, EF, GF, NF, SF)

I'll never forget the first time I enjoyed this marvelous and mouthwatering dish. It was a holiday, and my aunt Gloria made brisket for our family dinner. The brisket was a hit—particularly with my cousin Amy, who was 9½ months pregnant, and with me, who was 4 months along with my first.

I adopted and adapted my aunt's recipe to make it a bit easier to fit into my busy lifestyle. Are you surprised that her secret ingredient is a can of Coca-Cola®? The sugar in the soda will tenderize the meat and add a wonderful sweetness; and before you ask, for those reasons, do not use Diet Coke®.

While the brisket may take a couple hours to cook, you will only spend 5 minutes getting it in the oven or slow cooker, and then you can step away and enjoy the tantalizing aromas coming from your kitchen. Brace yourself for a life-changing brisket. It's the best of the best.

Prep Time: 5 minutes   Cook Time: 4 hours   Serves 6 to 8

Preheat the oven to 300°F (149°C).

Place the brisket in a disposable pan or slower cooker.

Sprinkle the onion soup mix over the brisket, and top with the chili sauce and ketchup. Add the mushrooms, if using, pour the Coca-Cola over everything, and add ½ cup (120 ml) of water.

Bake the brisket covered in the oven for 4 hours at 300°F (149°C), or in the slow cooker on low for 6 hours, until the meat is very tender.

Remove the brisket from the oven or slow cooker, and let the brisket come to room temperature before slicing. This takes about 30 minutes.

Cut the brisket against the grain before serving.

1 (3- to 4-pound [1.4- to 1.8-kg]) beef brisket

1 (1-ounce [27-g]) envelope onion soup mix (my favorite is Lipton Onion Soup Mix)

1 (12-ounce [340-ml]) bottle Heinz Chili Sauce

2 cups (480 ml) ketchup

1 (8-ounce [70-g]) package sliced mushrooms, optional

1 (8-ounce [237-ml]) can Coca-Cola

TIP: A butcher can show you how to cut brisket or any type of beef against the grain.

TERIYAKI BEEF SKEWERS

(DF, EF, GF, NF, SF)

Grab a bag! It's time to marinade! To me, the plastic resealable bag is one of the greatest inventions to benefit busy cooks. It's so easy to measure out a few ingredients, toss them in a bag, seal, shake and refrigerate! Give yourself a high five for being awesome, and head to bed. You'll sleep easier knowing that dinner is prepped and ready to go the following day.

My family and friends are superfans of these super tasty Teriyaki Beef Skewers. If your family loves them too, be sure to check out the Hawaiian Shoyu Chicken on page 35. Both recipes draw on the sweet-and-salty tang of teriyaki. In fact, they'd make great partners on the menu for a summer backyard luau. All you need are leis and drinks festooned with tiny umbrellas.

Prep Time: 5 minutes   Cook Time: 12 minutes   Serves 6

In a gallon-sized zip-top bag, combine the beef, soy sauce, brown sugar, pineapple juice, ginger and garlic. Seal the bag and shake to make sure that the meat is coated in the marinade.

Place the bag in the refrigerator for at least 2 hours or up to overnight.

Preheat the grill to low heat.

Remove the meat from the bag and thread the meat on metal skewers.

Grill the skewers for about 5 minutes on each side.

1½ pounds (680 g) boneless beef sirloin or flank steak, cut into ¼-inch (6-mm) slices

½ cup (120 ml) soy sauce, regular or gluten free

½ cup (110 g) light brown sugar

¼ cup (60 ml) pineapple juice (see Tips)

1 teaspoon ground ginger

2 cloves garlic, minced

TIPS: If you do not have pineapple juice on hand, you can use ¼ cup (60 ml) of honey.

If you are watching your salt intake, you should use low-sodium soy sauce.

HEARTY BEEF AND VEGGIE STEW

(DF, EF, GF, NF, SF)

This recipe dates back at least 15 years when I was on a kick of using my newly gifted slow cooker. At the bottom of the box was a stapled book of recipes. There was one for beef stew, and I thought, "Why not?" Believe me—that recipe included more than 6 minutes of prep, for sure! I was chopping, slicing and dicing. I was searing and using multiple pans. The stew turned out great, but even in those bygone days before kids, I needed a stew recipe with less prep and one pan. And, voilà! I created a way to make delicious beef stew without all the fuss.

Prep Time: 5 minutes   Cook Time: 2 hours   Serves 6

Preheat the oven to 300°F (149°C), and set a rack in the lower-middle position.

In a large Dutch oven, heat the oil over medium-high heat.

Add the cubed stew meat, and sear for about 3 minutes per side.

Remove the pot from the heat, and add the carrots, potatoes, tomato juice and beef broth. Stir everything together, and cover the pot.

Carefully put the pot in the oven, and cook for 2 hours or until the meat is very tender.

Remove from the oven, and season with salt to taste.

Alternatively, you can make this in the slow cooker: First sear the meat in a pan with the oil per the instructions above. Then add the meat, carrots, potatoes, tomato juice and beef broth to the slow cooker, and cook on low for 6 hours or high for 3 hours, until the meat is very tender.

2 tablespoons (30 ml) extra-virgin olive oil

2½ pounds (1.1 kg) beef stew meat, cubed

2 large carrots, peeled and diced

3 medium potatoes, diced

2 cups (480 ml) tomato juice

2 cups (480 ml) beef broth

TIP: Carrots and potatoes are my favorite veggies in the stew, but you can use other variations, such as peas, canned tomatoes or any of your favorites.

GRILLED LAMB CHOPS WITH MUSTARD RUB

(DF, EF, GF, LC, NF, SF)

Grilled lamb chops with mustard rub? So elegant and so easy! This recipe is one of my husband's absolute favorites. My sons love it, too! In fact, I've been doubling the recipe ever since my oldest entered adolescence and his never-ending appetite kicked in. Before long, I'll be tripling it.

When you make this recipe, you'll be following in the footsteps of the iconic Julia Child and her leg of lamb recipe, *Gigot à la Moutarde*. Sounds *très* fancy, right? Here's a secret—Julia used soy sauce in her marinade. She knew it was just the kick needed to elevate this dish from *bien* to *fantastique*! I love to serve this recipe to welcome spring. Brush the March snow off your grill, and *bon appétit*!

Prep Time: 5 minutes   Cook Time: 5 minutes   Serves 4

In a gallon-sized zip-top bag, combine the Dijon mustard, garlic and soy sauce. Seal the bag and shake to mix the ingredients.

Add the lamb chops to the bag and shake again to coat the lamb chops.

Marinate the lamb chops for several hours or up to overnight in the refrigerator.

When you're ready to grill, preheat the grill to medium heat. Remove the lamb chops from the marinade, and grill for 4 to 6 minutes on each side, depending on how well you want the meat to be done.

¼ cup (60 ml) Dijon mustard

2 cloves garlic, minced

¼ cup (60 ml) soy sauce

4 to 6 lamb shoulder or lamb loin chops (2 to 2½ pounds [907 g to 1.1 kg])

SMOKED BARBECUE BRISKET SLIDERS

(DF, NF, SF)

Several years ago, on a trip to the Smoky Mountains, we ordered smoked brisket sandwiches for the first time. When my husband took a bite, he looked at his sandwich the same way he had looked at me on our wedding night. Yes, it was that good. Was I jealous of that sandwich? Not really. However, my husband's happy face motivated me to replicate the recipe at home. The problem was that purchasing a smoker and tending to a brisket for a minimum of 12 labor-intensive hours did not exactly fit with the reality of being a busy mom. Liquid smoke to the rescue! After some trial and error, I finally perfected a recipe that transported our taste buds back to our first brisket sandwiches on that delicious Southern road trip. Your family and friends will definitely fall head over heels for these tantalizing sliders.

Prep Time: 5 minutes   Cook Time: 3 hours   Serves 8

Preheat the oven to 300°F (149°C).

Place the brisket in a large Dutch oven or slow cooker. Pour the liquid smoke, barbecue sauce, beer and Italian dressing over the brisket.

If using a Dutch oven, cover and bake for 3 hours until the brisket is very tender and easily pulls apart with a fork. If using a slow cooker, cook on high for 3 hours.

Using two forks, shred the brisket into bite-sized pieces.

Using a slotted spoon, scoop the brisket on the bottom halves of the rolls, dividing it evenly. Top with the top half of the roll and serve immediately.

1 (3-pound [1.4-kg]) first-cut beef brisket (see Tips)

2 tablespoons (30 ml) liquid smoke, such as Colgin All-Natural Hickory Liquid Smoke

1 cup (240 ml) barbecue sauce, such as Sweet Baby Ray's

½ bottle (6 oz [180 ml]) beer, such as Belgian ale

½ cup (120 ml) Italian salad dressing

8 to 10 Hawaiian rolls or brioche slider buns

TIPS: A first-cut brisket, also called the flat cut, is leaner than the second-cut brisket.

Add a slice of your favorite cheese or a spoonful of coleslaw to the brisket slider.

GRILLED LONDON BROIL WITH HONEY GLAZE

(DF, EF, GF, NF, SF)

London broil may bring to mind Big Ben, double-decker buses and some royal drama: What a load of poppycock! I don't mean to be cheeky, but this dish is 100 percent an American concoction, never to be found on a menu in the United Kingdom. "London broil" actually describes the way in which the meat is cooked—marinated, grilled and thinly sliced on the diagonal. Use this easy marinade to transform your cut into a perfectly tender piece of meat.

Is this dish worthy to serve to HRH the Queen of England? Yes. Yes, it is. And I'm not the only one who thinks so: It's the most popular dish on my blog, with views and shares totaling more than 150,000 and counting. You'll be the one wearing the crown when you serve it for dinner.

Prep Time: 5 minutes   Cook Time: 25 minutes   Serves 6

In a gallon-sized zip-top bag, mix the Italian dressing, soy sauce and honey.

Add the London broil to the bag, and let it marinate in the refrigerator for at least 3 hours or up to overnight.

When you're ready to grill, preheat a grill to low heat. Remove the beef from the marinade, and grill for 12 minutes on each side for medium (4 minutes longer per side if you like it well done).

Alternatively, you can cook the meat in the oven: Preheat the oven to 375°F (191°C), and bake the beef in a disposable pan uncovered on the lowest rack for 30 minutes (give or take 10 minutes depending on preferred level of doneness).

With this cut of meat, you want to let the meat sit covered for 5 to 10 minutes after cooking and before cutting to seal in the juices.

1 cup (240 ml) Italian salad dressing

¼ cup (60 ml) soy sauce, regular or gluten free

¼ cup (60 ml) honey

1 (1½- to 2-pound [681- to 907-kg]) London broil or flank steak

COUNTRY "FRIED" CHICKEN

(DF, GF, LC, NF, SF)

There's a special place in my heart for fried chicken—I love the crunchy skin and the tantalizing aroma. However, there's also a special place in my heart for, well, my heart. And my cholesterol level. And fitting into my pants for another year. So, I went on a cooking quest to create delicious "fried" chicken with less fat and fewer carbs, and ta-da! Here it is—one of the easiest and tastiest chicken dishes you'll ever make! The flavor is delicious, and the light coating of mayonnaise gives the outside a crispy texture that resembles fried chicken, but it's easy on the guilt and the carbs. Use leftover chicken breasts for lunches: They're perfect to serve on top of a green salad.

Prep Time: 5 minutes   Cook Time: 35 minutes   Serves 8

Preheat the oven to 375°F (191°C).

Arrange the chicken in a baking dish in a single layer, skin side up.

Rub the oil over the skin of the chicken, and sprinkle with seasoning salt. Spread the mayonnaise on top of the seasoning.

Bake uncovered for 35 to 40 minutes on the lower rack or until the internal temperature reads 165°F (74°C).

8 bone-in, skin-on chicken breasts

¼ cup (60 ml) extra-virgin olive oil

½ teaspoon seasoning salt

1 cup (240 ml) low-fat mayonnaise

TIP: If you like dark meat, you can substitute bone-in, skin-on chicken thighs.

CRISPY CORNFLAKE CHICKEN

(DF, EF, GF, NF, SF)

This is "Shake and Bake" à la Momma Chef. Kids love to help with the shaking step of this recipe, but be sure to keep their hands—and your hands—extra clean around raw chicken.

Our family prefers chicken breasts, but a follower of Momma Chef posted that she made this recipe with boneless, skinless chicken thighs, and her family loved it.

My kids typically go for the classic dipping sauce: ketchup! I like to mix it up by adding a second dipping sauce for variety. A current favorite is ½ cup (120 ml) of mayonnaise, ¼ cup (60 ml) of ketchup and a shake each of Worcestershire sauce, garlic powder and black pepper—YUM. Make the sauce ahead of time and chill it for several hours (or overnight!) in the refrigerator to maximize the flavor. Make this once, and it will become a favorite in your weekly menu rotation.

Prep Time: 5 minutes   Cook Time: 35 minutes   Serves 6

Preheat the oven to 375°F (191°C). Grease a baking sheet with nonstick spray.

Pour the Italian dressing into a large bowl.

In a gallon-sized zip-top bag, add the crushed cornflakes and salt.

Dip each chicken breast in the Italian dressing, then put them in the zip-top bag.

Shake to coat all sides of the chicken with the cornflake mixture.

Arrange the chicken in a single layer on the prepared baking sheet, and bake uncovered for 35 minutes or until the internal temperature reads 165°F (74°C).

½ cup (120 ml) zesty Italian salad dressing

4 cups (300 g) crushed cornflakes, regular or gluten free

1 teaspoon kosher salt

6 boneless, skinless chicken breasts

TIPS: If you prefer, in place of Italian dressing, you can use 2 eggs mixed with 1 tablespoon (15 ml) of water.

If you want to add a bit of sweetness, before baking, you can drizzle a bit of honey on the chicken. I suggest trying this with half of the chicken and seeing which one you like more.

HAWAIIAN SHOYU CHICKEN

(DF, EF, GF, NF, SF)

If you see me staring into nothingness with a goofy, contented smile on my face, I'm probably daydreaming about Hawaii. My family had the great fortune to vacation there recently. As promised, the islands were gorgeous and the food scrumptious. I fell in love with a traditional Hawaiian dish, the shoyu ahi poke bowl. It's sweet, it's salty, it's amazing and addictive. I knew my boys would love this flavor on chicken, so I created this version. Shoyu simply refers to a Japanese-style soy sauce. It provides a salty contrast to the sweetness of the pineapple and brown sugar. One whiff of the baking chicken's garlic-ginger aroma, and I'm transported back to paradise. Check out my favorite brand of soy sauce to use for this recipe in the Tips below.

Prep Time: 5 minutes   Cook Time: 35 minutes   Serves 6

In a gallon-sized zip-top bag, combine the chicken, soy sauce, pineapple and its juices, brown sugar, garlic and ginger, and shake to coat the chicken.

Place the bag in the refrigerator, and let the chicken marinate for 24 hours.

When you're ready to bake, preheat the oven to 375°F (191°C).

In a large, deep baking dish, add the chicken and the marinade, and arrange the chicken in a single layer, skin side up.

Bake the chicken uncovered for 35 to 40 minutes or until the internal temperature reads 165°F (74°C).

6 bone-in, skin-on chicken breasts

⅓ cup (80 ml) soy sauce, regular or gluten free

1 (8-ounce [227-g]) can crushed pineapple

⅓ cup (73 g) light brown sugar

2 teaspoons (3 g) minced garlic

1 teaspoon ground ginger

TIPS: I use the Aloha brand of soy sauce for this recipe. It's made in Hawaii and can be found online. The bottle lasts me months stored in the refrigerator.

When serving, I like to pour a little of the marinade and pineapple from the pan over the chicken and serve it with brown or white rice.

SZECHUAN CHICKEN STIR-FRY

(DF, EF, GF, LC, SF)

There's something about serving and eating stir-fry that just makes me feel good. Maybe it's because it's the best way to get all my kids to eat their veggies! Pre-kids, I made my fair share of "authentic" stir-fry dishes. Julienning peppers, chopping onions, cutting broccoli, slicing mushrooms, grating fresh ginger, mincing garlic and pounding chicken thin enough to cut it into strips? "That sounds manageable," said no busy human ever. This stir-fry recipe retains the hearty yum factor without the hearty time commitment.

If you're planning on serving rice, don't forget to start making it before you heat the wok. A rice cooker is by far the easiest way to cook perfect rice—just don't forget to push the start button! (This may seem obvious, yet I've missed this crucial step more than once!)

Prep Time: 5 minutes   Cook Time: 15 minutes   Serves 4

In a wok or large skillet, heat the oil over medium heat.

Add the chicken and garlic, and cook for about 5 minutes, stirring occasionally.

Add the vegetables and Szechuan sauce, and cook for another 8 to 10 minutes until the vegetables are soft.

Remove from the heat, and stir in the peanuts.

TIPS: You can ask your butcher or the meat department to cut the chicken for you, just request it be cut for stir-fry.

My personal favorite Szechuan sauce is San-J Szechuan Sauce (gluten free).

Do not use frozen vegetables in this dish; the vegetables will turn out soggy.

2 tablespoons (30 ml) extra-virgin olive oil or canola oil

1 pound (454 g) boneless, skinless chicken breasts, cut into cubes or strips (see Tips)

4 cloves garlic, chopped

½ cup (120 ml) Szechuan sauce (see Tips)

1 (10- to 12-ounce [283- to 340 g]) bag stir-fry blend vegetables (fresh, not frozen; see Tips)

⅓ cup (49 g) dry-roasted peanuts

HONEY-CURRY CHICKEN

(DF, EF, GF, NF, SF)

While your first inclination may be to skip over this recipe simply because it has curry in it, listen to me: do not be afraid. Once you make it, this recipe will become a top answer when you ask, "What should we have for dinner tonight?" The marinade is so scrumptious that even the pickiest eater will ask for seconds . . . and thirds. We like to spoon the "gravy" (the cooked marinade) from the bottom of the pan over rice or couscous—or even over a side of green beans. We've also been known to sneak a spoonful of the ambrosial goodness straight out of the pan!

The generous feedback I've received from the blogging community warms my heart, particularly when it comes from the most reluctant of cooks. It's consistently a variation of "Karen! I can't believe it! My whole family loves it!" Trust Momma Chef. Make this recipe tonight.

Prep Time: 5 minutes   Cook Time: 35 minutes   Serves 8

Preheat the oven to 375°F (191°C).

In a medium bowl, combine the honey, Dijon mustard, oil, curry powder and salt, and mix well.

In a 9 x 13-inch (23 x 33-cm) baking dish, add the chicken, and spread the honey-mustard mixture all over the chicken.

Arrange the chicken pieces in an even layer in the dish, skin side up.

Bake uncovered for 35 to 40 minutes until golden brown or the internal temperature reads 165°F (74°C).

If you like crispy skin, broil the chicken for the last 5 minutes until the skin has browned. Keep an eye on the chicken so you do not burn the skin.

¾ cup (180 ml) honey

¼ cup (60 ml) Dijon mustard

¼ cup (60 ml) extra-virgin olive oil

1 tablespoon (6 g) curry powder

1 teaspoon kosher salt

8 bone-in, skin-on chicken thighs

SHEET-PAN CHICKEN FAJITAS

(DF, EF, GF, LC, NF, SF)

In Chicagoland, we have our pick of some of the best authentic Mexican cuisine. But, back in the 1980s, we were all agog with a new-fangled Tex-Mex chain restaurant, Chi-Chis. Margaritas as big as your head. Fried ice cream. Chimichangas. Oversized birthday sombreros. You get it. It was there that I experienced my first encounter with fajitas. A server strolled past our table balancing a tray of them, crackling and steaming with the most delicioso aroma. Oy! I just had to try them! When my order arrived, I was super jazzed by all the special accoutrements that accompanied it: my own tortilla warmer, teeny-tiny tongs, sides of sour cream and salsa, and the tour de force—a cast-iron pan, sizzling with chicken, peppers and onions. While the novelty of the restaurant eventually waned, my love for fajitas stayed strong. Here's a fabulous way to serve up this delicious meal—and all in one pan!

Prep Time: 5 minutes   Cook Time: 20 minutes   Serves 6

Preheat the oven to 400°F (204°C).

Generously coat a baking sheet with cooking spray.

In a gallon-sized zip-top bag, add the chicken, red and yellow peppers, onion and fajita seasoning. Seal and shake the bag so the chicken and vegetables are coated in the fajita seasoning.

Pour everything from the bag onto the prepared baking sheet, and spread the chicken and vegetables in a single layer.

Bake uncovered for 20 to 25 minutes until the chicken is cooked through.

Remove from the oven, and squeeze the lime over the chicken and vegetables. Serve immediately.

1½ pounds (681 g) boneless, skinless chicken breast, cut into ½-inch (1.3-cm) strips (see Tips)

1 red pepper, cored and sliced

1 yellow pepper, cored and sliced

½ yellow onion, sliced

1 (1- to 1½-ounce [28- to 42-g]) package fajita seasoning

½ fresh lime

TIPS: You can ask your butcher or the meat department to cut the chicken for you, just request it be cut in strips for stir-fry.

You can usually find fresh, precut strips of peppers in the grocery store; you want to use about 2 full cups (300 g) of sliced assorted peppers.

ZESTY LEMON-HERB CHICKEN

(DF, EF, GF, LC, NF, SF)

This delicious dish got its start after a long day of carpooling. As I was driving home, I mentally reviewed what was in my house to make for dinner. Beyond the chicken that was thawing in the refrigerator, the answer was, "Not a lot, Karen. Not a lot." Fortunately, it was summertime, and my herb garden was flourishing. I grabbed a few handfuls from several plants and created this tasty marinade. Its flavor profile is simple enough that even the pickiest of eaters will love it—yet it's elegant enough that you can serve it for a dinner party. Having your own herb garden, by the way, will save you money, make your food tastier and help you be a happier human. Don't be intimidated: Herb gardens are far more manageable than vegetable gardens. Herbs can be grown in pots, indoors or outdoors. Caution: once you develop a taste for fresh herbs, there'll be no turning back.

Prep Time: 5 minutes   Cook Time: 35 minutes   Serves 6

Preheat the oven to 375°F (191°C).

In a mixing bowl, combine the lemon juice, oil, fresh herbs, salt and garlic.

Place the chicken skin side up evenly around a 9 x 13-inch (23 x 33-cm) baking dish, and pour the marinade over the chicken (I use disposable gloves and try to stuff some of the marinade under the skin).

You can also slice one of the squeezed lemons and put it around the dish for extra flavor.

Bake uncovered for 35 to 40 minutes until golden brown and the internal temperature reads 165°F (74°C).

If you like crispy skin, broil the chicken for the last 5 minutes until the skin has browned; just keep an eye on the chicken so the skin does not burn.

Juice of 2 lemons (or ⅓ cup [80 ml] lemon juice)

¼ cup (60 ml) extra-virgin olive oil

¼ cup (15 g) chopped fresh herbs, such as basil, rosemary, parsley or oregano

2 teaspoons (12 g) kosher salt

4 cloves garlic, chopped

6 bone-in, skin-on chicken thighs or breasts

ROASTED BEER-CAN CHICKEN

(DF, EF, GF, LC, NF, SF)

I live in a house chock-full of boys and have become well versed in typical boy humor. Belching? They'll definitely think that's funny. Flatulence? Hysterical. I knew that all I had to do was tell my sons the alternate name of this popular dish—"Beer Butt Chicken"—and they'd immediately be fans.

The first time I made this, I failed to secure the can properly, and my poor chicken toppled over, humiliated in a puddle of beer. Fortunately, it still tasted great. I've learned to double-check the stability of the can and to do a mid-bake oven check to make sure the chicken doesn't get tipsy. If you don't like the taste of beer, no worries. The beer evaporates into the cavity of the chicken while it's cooking, making the chicken unbelievably moist and flavorful.

Prep Time: 5 minutes   Cook Time: 1 hour 30 minutes   Serves 6

Preheat the oven to 375°F (191°C). Place the rack in the lowest position in the oven.

Rub the chicken inside and out with the oil, seasoning salt and rotisserie seasoning.

Pour half of the beer into the bottom of a deep baking dish.

Place the open beer can with the remaining beer in the center of the baking dish, and carefully place the chicken over the beer can with the legs on the bottom.

Bake uncovered for 1 hour 30 minutes, checking occasionally that the chicken is still standing up over the beer can.

> **TIP:** If you use a smaller or larger chicken, make sure to adjust the cooking time. On average, allow 20 minutes of cooking time per pound or until the internal temperature reads 165°F (74°C).

1 whole chicken, about 4 pounds (1.8 kg)

1 tablespoon (15 ml) extra-virgin olive oil

1 tablespoon (18 g) seasoning salt

2 tablespoons (36 g) rotisserie chicken seasoning, such as McCormick

1 (12-ounce [355-ml]) can of beer (if making gluten free, use a gluten-free beer)

DOWN-HOME CHICKEN AND RICE CASSEROLE

(DF, EF, GF, NF, SF)

Maine rocks the lobster roll; New Orleans owns the gumbo; and the Midwest? We are all about the casserole. American casseroles are magical mixtures, traditionally baked and served in rectangular Pyrex dishes. No matter the ingredients, a true casserole's components work together to produce a calming concoction with a 1:1 ratio of "yum" to "comfort." It's essentially a warm hug in a pan.

Here, chicken and rice—the darlings of the casserole world—perfectly pair together, joined by a savory base. You'll love how easy it is to incorporate a vegetable into this meal. Below, I prepared the recipe with peas. You could switch them out for frozen carrots or frozen corn (or try a combination of all three). This casserole is my go-to to keep my family warm and satisfied on chilly winter nights.

Prep Time: 5 minutes   Cook Time: 1 hour   Serves 6

Preheat the oven to 400°F (204°C).

In a small pot, add the chicken broth, and bring to a boil.

Remove from the heat, and in a 9 x 13-inch (23 x 22-cm) baking dish, combine the hot chicken broth, rice and peas.

Place the chicken breasts over the rice mixture, and sprinkle the onion soup mix over the chicken.

Cover the pan tightly with foil, and bake covered until all the liquid is absorbed, about 1 hour. Make sure the pan is covered tightly so the rice will cook.

4 cups (960 ml) chicken broth

1½ cups (300 g) long-grain white rice

1 (12-oz [340-g]) bag frozen peas

6 boneless, skinless chicken breasts

1 (1-ounce [28-g]) packet onion soup mix (my favorite is Lipton Onion Soup Mix)

LET THEM EAT FISH

Every New Year, one of my resolutions invariably includes feeding my family more fish. It can be a tough sell. And obviously, not just at my house. Experts recommend adults eat 26 pounds (11.8 kg) of fish per year; Americans eat half that, at most. Meanwhile, we annually clock in at an average of 222 pounds (100.8 kg) of meat per person. I'm trying to slowly change this trend, one delicious fish recipe at a time.

What's so great about fish? It's tough to ignore the crazy nutritional benefits of omega-3 fatty acids, abundantly found in many fish. What other food legitimately makes our brains work better? Staves off memory loss? Lowers heart disease and stroke? The more I read about its scientifically proven health benefits, my brain nearly explodes. *Why aren't I eating fish every darn day?* The good news is that we can reap the positive health benefits by incorporating fish into our diets once or twice a week. The bad news is that I feel like an overachiever if I serve fish once or twice a month.

My kids are getting old enough now that they can participate a bit more in the larger discussion of fish as a responsible, sustainable use of our natural resources. Thanks to social media (for real), they seem to have a better awareness of how our choices—like eating green—impact our world.

Despite my kids' increasing global awareness, when fish is on the menu, they aren't running to the table like they do when I'm serving up Smoked Barbecue Brisket Sliders (page 27) or Three-Ingredient Chicken Wings (page 94). I do have some tricks up my sleeve to get them on board, though. In every case, *looks matter*! Coconut-Curry Mahi-Mahi (page 55) looked so lovely that my kids were willing to give it a try, and guess what? They're fans! Spicy Fish Kebabs (page 56) were an easy sell as well—just call the skewers "lightsabers" and the (fish) force will be with you.

The fish department at your local grocery store can be a huge help in making these dinners even easier. Ask them to make sure the fish is deboned. They will take off the skin if you wish or prep the fish for whichever dish you are making, for example, cut the mahi-mahi into 1-inch (2.5-cm) cubes.

Love to squeeze lemon on your fish? Here's my favorite trick: cut a lemon in half, and heat it in the microwave for 30 seconds (or until warm). Not only are warmed lemons much easier to squeeze, you will get almost double the juice!

LEMON-HERB SALMON

(DF, EF, GF, LC, NF, SF)

Want to cook a fabulous weeknight meal and make your family smarter? Choose salmon, the DHA darling of the sea. DHA is all kinds of good news for our brains—boosting memory, improving cognitive functioning and staving off depression. In nonscientific terms: eat more salmon. This recipe tops the list with its sweet-and-spicy flavor profile. Here, I use a Mediterranean-style marinade with a strong lemon base. You'll love how it balances the sweetness of the brown sugar and the bite of the chili powder.

My number one tip here: use a timer. This salmon will be A+ perfect after baking for 20 minutes on the dot. (See the Tips below to see how serious I am about the sanctity of the 20 minutes!)

Prep Time: 5 minutes   Cook Time: 20 minutes   Serves 4 to 6

Preheat the oven to 375°F (191°C).

Coat a 9 x 13-inch (23 x 33-cm) baking dish with cooking spray, and place the salmon fillet skin side down in the dish.

In a small bowl, whisk together the brown sugar, salt and chili powder. Rub the spice mixture all over the top of the salmon.

Pour the marinade evenly over the salmon. Bake uncovered until the salmon is cooked through, 20 minutes. Serve warm.

1½- to 2-pound (681- to 907-g) salmon fillet

1 tablespoon (14 g) packed light brown sugar

1 teaspoon kosher salt

½ teaspoon chili powder

¼ cup (60 ml) Mediterranean-style herb marinade, such as Lawry's Mediterranean Herb & White Wine marinade

TIPS: If you can't find the Mediterranean marinade, you can make your own using ¼ cup (60 ml) of extra-virgin olive oil, 1 teaspoon of dried basil and 1 tablespoon (15 ml) of lemon juice.

The "20 minutes on the dot" is serious business. Let's say, just as the 20-minute timer beeps, you hear your children screaming from the basement, "Mom! Mom! [your potty-training son] is peeing on the carpet!" What would you do? A) Pause and take out the salmon or B) Go deal with the basement piddling stat? It's a no-brainer: You take the salmon *out*. True story, friends. True story.

MOROCCAN FISH WITH CHICKPEAS

(DF, EF, GF, NF, SF)

If you have some fish-hesitant eaters, tilapia can serve as the perfect gateway fish to becoming a seafood addict. It's mildly flavored and comparatively less expensive than other seafood. While you can buy tilapia fresh from the seafood counter, I often buy a bag of frozen fillets as they're perfect to have on hand. This dish pairs delightfully with Israeli Couscous with Sautéed Onions (see page 143).

Should you go all out and host a multicourse meal, this recipe makes an elegant choice as an appetizer. It looks amazing served on colorful, tiny dishes—maybe the ones that you impulsively bought at World Market three years ago but haven't used since.

Prep Time: 5 minutes   Cook Time: 15 minutes   Serves 6

In a large saucepan, heat the olive oil over medium heat. Add the garlic, and sauté for 3 minutes. Add the tomato paste, all-seasons salt and 2 cups (480 ml) of water.

Mix everything together so the tomato paste becomes liquid.

Lightly lay the tilapia fillets over the sauce, spooning some of the sauce to cover the fillets.

Add in the chickpeas, and cover the pot. Reduce the heat to medium-low, and cook covered for 15 minutes.

Remove from the heat.

¼ cup (60 ml) extra-virgin olive oil

5 cloves garlic, chopped

1 (6-ounce [177-ml]) can tomato paste

2 teaspoons (12 g) all-seasons salt

6 (4-ounce [113-g]) tilapia fillets (see Tips)

1 (15.5-ounce [439-g]) can chickpeas, drained and rinsed

> **TIPS:** You can use other fish in the recipe, such as whitefish, red snapper or rainbow trout.
>
> My family likes this dish spicy, so I add in ½ teaspoon of chili flakes when adding in the chickpeas.

COCONUT-CURRY MAHI-MAHI

(DF, EF, GF, LC, NF, SF)

Mahi-mahi! It's not only fun to say, it's delicious to eat. Just ask my youngest son. He was none too happy when I first set this dish on the dinner table. Knowing he doesn't love fish, I was prepared, armed with Parenting Trick #774: The "Single Bite" Stipulation—"Just one bite, and if you don't like it, you don't have to eat it." He skeptically took a bite. And then a second. And a third. I loved how obviously pleased he was that he'd tried something new and really liked it.

Mahi-mahi is a firm, meaty fish, and its sweet, mild flavor makes it a versatile favorite. We call it "fin-tastic!" at our house—particularly my youngest son and proud mahi-mahi convert.

Prep Time: 5 minutes   Cook Time: 15 minutes   Serves 4

In a large skillet, heat the oil over medium-high heat. Stir in the garlic, and cook for about 2 minutes.

Add the curry paste, coconut milk and brown sugar to the skillet. Mix and cook for 3 minutes more.

Add the mahi-mahi to the pan, and gently spoon the curry mixture over the fish.

Cover the skillet, and cook for 10 minutes.

Remove from the heat, and serve immediately.

2 tablespoons (30 ml) melted coconut oil

3 cloves garlic, crushed

3 tablespoons (45 ml) red Thai curry paste

1 (14-ounce [400-ml]) can coconut milk

1 tablespoon (14 g) light brown sugar

1½ pounds (681 g) mahi-mahi, cut into 1-inch (2.5-cm) cubes (see Tip)

TIP: If you want an alternative to mahi-mahi, you can substitute salmon, cod or halibut.

SPICY FISH KEBABS

(DF, EF, GF, LC, NF, SF)

Kebabs are kind of my thing. (Don't miss the Teriyaki Beef Skewers on page 20 and the Beef Kebabs on Cinnamon Sticks on page 12.) And doubling down on the spice? That's kind of my family's thing. Here, harissa, a Middle Eastern and North African paste, adds spice and layers of flavor to the fish marinade. These few ingredients produce the best-tasting kebabs you'll ever eat. When making the kebabs, if you don't have metal skewers and are opting for wooden ones, be sure and soak them in water for at least 30 minutes prior to cooking. Otherwise, your kebabs can catch on fire—and fish aren't well known for their stop, drop and roll skills.

Prep Time: 5 minutes   Cook Time: 10 minutes   Serves 5

In a gallon-sized zip-top bag, add the salmon, oil, sea salt and harissa. Carefully shake to coat the salmon.

Place the zip-top bag in the refrigerator, and let the fish marinate for at least 1 hour or up to 8 hours.

Remove the fish from the refrigerator, and thread the fish and red onion pieces onto the skewers, alternating the fish and onion.

Preheat the grill to medium-low. Grill the kebabs for 5 to 6 minutes per side, until the fish is done to your liking.

1½ pounds (681 g) salmon fillet, cut into 1-inch (2.5-cm) chunks

2 tablespoons (30 ml) extra-virgin olive oil

1½ teaspoons (9 g) sea salt

2 tablespoons (30 ml) harissa

1 large red onion, cut into chunks

BLACKENED RED SNAPPER

(DF, EF, GF, LC, NF, SF)

The 1980s introduced us to MTV, Cabbage Patch Dolls, *The Breakfast Club*, crimped hair, and . . . Cajun blackened fish? Like, totally! In the spring of 1980, New Orleans chef Paul Prudhomme first served blackened redfish to a small crowd at his restaurant. By the end of the month, diners were lined up around the block. Today, it seems as though blackening has always been around. You can order blackened fish, chicken, steak and vegetables.

To me, fish is hands down the best way to enjoy the big, bold flavors of blackening, and this recipe is the best of the best. When serving the finished fillets, don't forget the lemon! It provides a fresh and zesty zing—plus, my kids love to squeeze the wedges over their dinner.

Prep Time: 5 minutes   Cook Time: 10 minutes   Serves 4

Using paper towels, pat dry the red snapper fillets.

In a small bowl, mix together the salt and blackened seasoning.

Season both sides of the snapper fillets with the salt and blackened seasoning mixture.

In a frying pan, heat the oil over medium heat. (The pan should be large enough that all fillets can cook at once without touching.) Swirl the pan to make sure the oil coats the entire bottom of the pan.

Add the fillets to the pan, flesh side down.

Cook uncovered for 4 minutes. Then, with a sturdy spatula, carefully flip the fillets and cook the skin side for another 3 minutes.

Carefully remove the fish from the pan, and serve with the lemon wedges.

4 (6-ounce [170-g]) red snapper fillets (see Tip)

1 teaspoon kosher or sea salt

3 tablespoons (15 g) blackened seasoning, such as Louisiana Cajun Blackened Seasoning

3 tablespoons (45 ml) canola or avocado oil

½ lemon, cut into wedges

TIP: You can use this recipe for other fish, such as whitefish, grouper, haddock and tilapia.

MISO-GLAZED COD

(DF, EF, NF, SF)

This has to be one of the easiest—and most succulent—fish dishes to make. At the iconic Nobu restaurant, black cod with miso is prominently featured as one of the favorite dishes of internationally renowned chef Nobuyuki Matsuhisa. While the price of black cod may be higher than other fish, it's worth it. Relatively, it's an absolute bargain when compared to ordering it at a restaurant!

Plus, black cod's high-fat content equals a high omega-3 content (the highest among whitefish), giving you all those brain benefits. Even if you're new to the fish-cooking game, relax. You absolutely cannot mess up this recipe. It's foolproof and fabulous. You'll find that this recipe converts even the most reticent of fish eaters at first bite.

Prep Time: 5 minutes   Cook Time: 10 minutes   Serves 4

For the marinade, in a large microwave-safe bowl, whisk together the miso paste, mirin, sake and brown sugar.

Cook the marinade in the microwave for 2 minutes until most of the sugar is dissolved, stirring to combine.

Add the cod to the bowl, and rub the marinade over both sides.

If possible, marinate the cod in the refrigerator for 1 to 2 hours.

Preheat the oven to broil, letting the oven heat up for about 10 minutes. Line a sheet pan with aluminum foil.

When you're ready to bake, place the cod fillets on the prepared sheet pan.

Broil the fish uncovered for 8 to 9 minutes until the fillets are fork tender and caramelized.

Make sure to keep an eye on your fish while it is broiling. You want the top to be golden brown with a hint of black but not charred.

¼ cup (60 ml) miso paste

⅓ cup (80 ml) mirin (Japanese cooking wine)

¼ cup (60 ml) cooking sake

3 tablespoons (42 g) light brown sugar

4 (6-ounce [170-g]) black cod fillets

WHITEFISH IN CAPER-WHITE WINE SAUCE

(DF, EF, GF, LC, NF, SF)

One fish, two fish. Red fish, blue fish. And whitefish! Lots and lots of whitefish. Here's a favorite way that this Illinois girl likes to prepare whitefish harvested from the nearby Great Lakes for my family. The capers, lemon juice and white wine combine to make one of the best whitefish recipes you'll ever make. Be sure to use a good white wine for the sauce—and be certain to set aside a glass or two for the cook.

For this recipe as well as for the others in this chapter, I strongly suggest purchasing a fish turner for the best success with this tender, flaky fish. Even if you don't ever plan on making fish more than once a year, it's a worthy $15 investment.

Prep Time: 5 minutes   Cook Time: 10 minutes   Serves 4

Using paper towels, pat dry the whitefish fillets.

In a large nonstick frying pan, melt the butter over medium heat. Swirl the pan to make sure the butter coats the entire bottom of the pan.

Add the fillets, flesh side down, to the pan, and cook for 3 minutes on each side, carefully flipping with a sturdy spatula.

While the fillets are cooking, in a small saucepan, add the wine, lemon juice, parsley and capers.

Cook over medium heat for 5 minutes.

Carefully plate the fish, pour the white wine sauce over the fish, and serve immediately.

4 (6-ounce [170-g]) whitefish fillets (see Tip)

3 tablespoons (42 g) salted butter or margarine

1 cup (240 ml) dry white wine

3 tablespoons (45 ml) lemon juice

¼ cup (15 g) chopped fresh flat-leaf parsley

¼ cup (30 g) capers, drained

TIP: You can use tilapia, cod, bass, grouper, haddock or snapper in this recipe in place of whitefish.

BROILED LEMON-SOY ARCTIC CHAR

(DF, EF, GF, NF, SF)

If you've never met before, allow me to introduce you to Arctic char. It's a lovely fish, similar in color and texture to salmon. Arctic char is plentiful, sustainable and affordable—and it even has those wonderful omega-3 fatty acids that science is agog over. It's a win-win-win-win.

You'll find that the flavor of Arctic char is somewhere between salmon and trout, leaning toward trout. Its delicate taste makes it the perfect vehicle for the delicious flavors of lemon, honey, garlic and soy. With this savory marinade, you'll enjoy this fish to the last little browned nugget at the bottom of the pan.

Prep Time: 5 minutes   Cook Time: 20 minutes   Serves 6

Preheat the oven to 375°F (191°C).

Coat a 9 x 13–inch (23 x 22–cm) baking dish with cooking spray, and place the Arctic char skin side down in the dish.

In a small mixing bowl, whisk together the honey, lemon juice, soy sauce and garlic.

Pour the marinade evenly over the fish.

Bake uncovered until the fish is cooked through, about 20 minutes.

Plate with the sliced lemons.

2-pound (907-g) skinless Arctic char fillet (see Tips)

½ cup (120 ml) honey

¼ cup (60 ml) lemon juice

¼ cup (60 ml) soy sauce, regular or gluten free

2 cloves garlic, chopped

1 lemon, cut into 8 slices

TIPS: You can use salmon or trout in this recipe in place of Arctic char.

Because of the honey, this marinade can stick to the pan and make cleanup difficult, so I like to make this in a disposable half pan.

RISE AND SHINE

Here's a typical morning in Momma Chef's home:

The alarm sounds, but no worries, for I have arisen early for yoga and meditation. Outside, animated songbirds sweetly sing, while inside, I hear my three sons greeting the day with friendly banter. We all head to our spotless kitchen where we work in harmony to make a healthy breakfast to nourish our bodies and souls for the day. They hug me goodbye, and—

BEEP! BEEP! BEEP! My real alarm jolts me to reality as that ridiculous dream evaporates. Getting three kids out of bed and then out the door with permission slips signed, computers charged, homework completed and (mostly) matching clothes is a daily challenge. Add a nourishing breakfast to this carnival? Sometimes it would just be easier to throw them a toaster pastry or a handful of Halloween candy.

If your morning routines are more closely aligned with my family's typical A.M. chaos, the recipes here are designed to make homemade breakfasts manageable. Check out this chapter's grab-and-go muffins and make-ahead dishes to start everyone's day on the right foot. Try the scrumptious Kid-Approved Healthy Blueberry Muffins (page 82) and the Hidden Zucchini Muffins (page 89). They're not only delicious for breakfast, they're also a fabulous pick-me-up before an afternoon soccer practice or orchestra rehearsal. If you're looking to reap the benefits of a protein-packed start to the day, choose the Grab-and-Go Breakfast Egg Muffins (page 69). I make these at least once a week, if not more. The secret is that you can change them up with whichever veggies and protein you have on hand.

You'll also find recipes here for more leisurely weekend breakfasts and brunches. To me, the most important part of brunch is being together—strengthening relationships and celebrating one another. That's why I've chosen delicious recipes that will give you the time to be fully present at the table instead of rushing back and forth to the kitchen.

My absolute favorite brunch recipe is The Famous Blintz Soufflé (page 86), forever made best by my mom. A recent family favorite is the Brioche French Toast Casserole (page 74). It's best stirred up the night before. As it bakes, the caramelized aroma will welcome family and friends (and my dog—always my dog) into the kitchen.

May these breakfast recipes bring you peace on your busy mornings and pleasure as you gather around the brunch table.

GRAB-AND-GO BREAKFAST EGG MUFFINS

(GF, LC, NF, SF, V)

Mornings + kids = chaos. Here's a simple way to help start your day happier and healthier. Whip up a batch of these savory muffins on Sunday night, and you'll have a week of easy breakfasts for your kids as they scramble (get it?) for the school bus. These lifesavers last several days in the refrigerator. Just heat them in the microwave for 25 seconds, and you're Mom of the Year. Another bonus? You can customize them with your leftovers. Add any cheese, veggies and meat you have in your refrigerator. My boys are big fans of broccoli and Cheddar cheese.

Prep Time: 5 minutes   Cook Time: 20 minutes   Makes 12 muffins

Preheat the oven to 375°F (191°C).

Coat a standard 12-cup muffin pan with cooking spray.

In a medium bowl, lightly beat together the eggs, milk and salt, and set aside.

Divide the vegetables and cheese among the muffin cups.

Pour the egg mixture into each muffin cup over the vegetables and cheese, filling each one about three-quarters full.

Bake uncovered until golden brown and cooked through, about 20 minutes.

6 eggs

2 tablespoons (30 ml) whole milk

½ teaspoon kosher salt

½ cup chopped fresh vegetables, such as broccoli or spinach

¼ cup (28 g) shredded cheese, such as sharp Cheddar

TIPS: The vegetables do not need to be cooked before adding them to the muffin pan. The only exception is onions; if you are going to be using these, I would suggest sautéing them for 3 minutes before adding them to the recipe.

Try adding some fresh herbs, such as fresh chopped basil or dill.

If you have picky breakfast eaters, let them choose the veggies and cheese, and have them put the ingredients in the muffin cup. It's an easy and fun way for kids to "cook"! Plus, kids are excited to try the foods that they cook themselves.

MARVELOUS FOUR-INGREDIENT NUTELLA CREPES

(NF, SF, V)

If you've ever been intimidated by making crepes, you won't be after trying this four-ingredient recipe! The blender is the trick to making (and pouring) perfect crepes. You'll be crowned Best Parent Ever if you serve these to your kids' friends after a sleepover. (They're a perfect treat after an adult sleepover, too!) Serve with a sliced banana or some strawberries to balance out this rich treat. Looking for a savory crepe? Check out the Tips below.

Prep Time: 5 minutes   Cook Time: 5 minutes   Makes 8 crepes

In a blender, combine the flour, milk and eggs, and blend until smooth. You can also mix this in a large bowl using a whisk or hand mixer.

Coat a small 8- to 10-inch (20- to 25-cm) frying pan generously with cooking spray, and heat over medium heat.

Once the pan is hot, pour ¼ cup (60 ml) of the batter into the pan, making sure the entire pan is coated with the batter (if there are spots that are not coated, you can add more batter to those spots).

Cook until the edges pull off the pan, about 2 minutes, then flip and cook 2 minutes more. Both sides should be very lightly brown. Remove from the heat, and spread 1 tablespoon (16 g) of Nutella in the center of the crepe.

After the crepe is filled, fold over one side on top of the filling, then fold over the other side on top to close the crepe.

2 cups (250 g) all-purpose flour

2½ cups (600 ml) whole milk

2 eggs

8 tablespoons (128 g) Nutella®

> **TIPS:** Other filling ideas: chocolate spread, Nutella and strawberries or bananas, sautéed mushrooms and onions with a dash of salt, sautéed spinach and tomato, scrambled eggs with salsa . . . the possibilities are endless.
>
> You can make this recipe dairy free by using almond or rice milk and dairy-free chocolate-hazelnut spread.
>
> This batter will stay good in an airtight container in the refrigerator for up to 3 days. Just give the batter a quick stir when you're ready to make the crepes.

CRISPY HASH BROWN CASSEROLE

(EF, GF, NF, SF, V)

Here, an iconic Midwestern comfort food acts as a hearty side dish for both brunch and dinner. The crispy topping contrasts perfectly with the creamy, cheesy potato mixture. I like to double the recipe to ensure we have leftovers. If you're making this ahead for a special occasion, you may want to hide this in the back of the refrigerator, away from the prying eyes of the snack scavengers at your house. While some people indulge in a bowl of ice cream, I would rather splurge on a late-night warm scoop of this scrumptious carb-fest. Go ahead—treat yourself to a little guilty pleasure.

Don't lose the crunch if you eat gluten free! Replace the cornflakes with Rice Chex or gluten-free Rice Krispies.

Prep Time: 5 minutes   Cook Time: 40 minutes   Serves 8

Preheat the oven to 350°F (177°C).

In a large bowl, stir together the hash browns, cheese, mushroom soup, salt and sour cream until thoroughly combined.

Coat a 9 x 13–inch (23 x 33–cm) baking dish with cooking spray, and pour the hash brown mixture into the dish.

Sprinkle the crushed cornflakes over the mixture.

Bake uncovered until the cheese is bubbling, 40 to 45 minutes. Let it rest for 5 to 10 minutes before serving.

> **TIP:** I like to take the frozen hash browns out the night before and let them defrost overnight in the refrigerator.

2 pounds (907 g) frozen hash browns, thawed

2 cups (224 g) shredded Cheddar cheese

1 (10½-ounce [298-g]) can cream of mushroom soup

1 teaspoon kosher salt

1 cup (240 ml) sour cream

2 cups (150 g) cornflakes, crushed (if making gluten free, use Rice Chex)

BRIOCHE FRENCH TOAST CASSEROLE

(NF, SF, V)

I dedicate this Mother's Day recipe to all the great moms out there, especially my mom! My mom has passed on a lot to me: her blue eyes, her love of family fun, and the ability to walk the fine line between pure Momma Love and overprotective neuroticism. Think Beverly Goldberg minus the shoulder pads—although she *still* might come over sporting a 1980s jumpsuit with big white Reebok® shoes. I know that I have crossed over to my mom's level of neuroticism when my kids affectionately start calling me "Bev."

French toast is fabulous, but standing in front of a skillet for 30 minutes making ten pieces of French toast is not a treat for anyone, especially a mom on Mother's Day. That's why I love this recipe: you (or your minions) can prep it in 5 minutes and pop it in the oven.

Prep Time: 5 minutes   Cook Time: 40 minutes   Serves 8

Preheat the oven to 350°F (177°C), and adjust a rack to the lower third of the oven.

Slice the brioche bread into 1-inch (2.5-cm) slices, and then cut those into 1-inch (2.5-cm) cubes.

Pour the melted butter into a 9 x 13–inch (23 x 33–cm) baking dish, and tilt the dish to coat well.

Layer the bread in the baking dish.

In a medium bowl, whisk together the milk, eggs, brown sugar and vanilla, and pour this mixture evenly over the bread.

Bake uncovered for 40 to 45 minutes, or until a toothpick comes out clean.

Remove from the oven, and let it sit for 5 to 10 minutes before serving.

1 (14- to 16-ounce [397- to 454-g]) loaf brioche bread (see Tip)

2 tablespoons (28 ml) melted unsalted butter

2 cups (480 ml) whole or 2 percent milk

6 eggs

½ cup (110 g) light brown sugar

1 teaspoon (5 ml) vanilla extract

TIP: You can substitute brioche bread with a soft challah bread.

GLUTEN-FREE BANANA MUFFINS

(DF, GF, NF, SF, V)

I was asked to teach a cooking class for kids, and one of our campers was gluten intolerant. Rather than completely eliminating baked goods from our culinary curriculum, I researched how to alter my favorite recipe to make sure everyone had the chance to be muffin men. I was delighted to find that if I simply substitute with a 1-to-1 flour, such as Bob's Red Mill Gluten-Free 1-to-1 Baking Flour, I can keep my favorite recipe as is. That week, my cooking apprentices were excited to put on their aprons and to tackle this recipe. The final result? Everyone in the class devoured them! I'm sure they will become a favorite at your house as well. You'll want to have a batch ready in the freezer should one of your gluten-free friends stop over for coffee.

Prep Time: 5 minutes   Cook Time: 20 minutes   Makes 12 muffins

Preheat the oven to 375°F (191°C).

In a large mixing bowl, add the gluten-free flour, bananas, eggs, baking soda, honey and oil, and blend with a hand mixer on medium speed for about 3 minutes.

Divide the batter into 12 greased (I use cooking spray) or paper-lined muffin cups.

Bake uncovered for 15 to 20 minutes until a toothpick inserted into the center comes out clean.

1½ cups (189 g) gluten-free 1-to-1 baking flour

3 overripe bananas

2 eggs

1 teaspoon baking soda

½ cup (120 ml) honey

⅓ cup (80 ml) avocado oil

TIPS: These muffins make a great holiday gift for someone gluten free; just package the muffins in a cute gift box.

I like to freeze the muffins individually in small zip-top bags for guests who stop over who are gluten free. Just defrost them for 30 seconds in the microwave before serving. They will stay good in the freezer for up to 3 months.

If you don't have anyone gluten free in your household, you can use all-purpose flour.

POTATO, SPINACH AND GOAT CHEESE FRITTATA

(GF, NF, SF, V)

You're going to be amazed at how few ingredients and little time it takes to prepare this delicious and satisfying dish. And don't let the fancy-sounding name intimidate you. It's not just for sophisticated palates. My boys can't get enough of it. Just like the other egg dishes in this chapter, you'll love its flexibility. Personalize this dish with your favorites: broccoli and scallions, red pepper and mozzarella, or whatever is in your vegetable crisper. You can also use a cast-iron skillet to bake this, but I've found a simple pie dish works just as well. You could easily add this recipe to your dinner rotation; pair it with a crisp green salad and a glass of white wine. Or two. Momma Chef knows there are days like that.

Prep Time: 5 minutes   Cook Time: 35 minutes   Serves 8

Preheat the oven to 350°F (177°C).

In a large bowl, add the eggs, and blend with a hand mixer on low speed for about 2 minutes.

Add the milk, potatoes, spinach and garlic salt, and blend for another 30 seconds.

Coat a pie dish with cooking spray, and pour the egg mixture into the dish.

Crumble the goat cheese over the mixture.

Bake uncovered for 35 minutes, or until the eggs are set in the middle.

8 eggs

½ cup (120 ml) whole milk

1 cup (150 g) red potatoes, cubed

1 cup (30 g) chopped spinach

1 teaspoon garlic salt or kosher salt

⅓ cup (74 g) goat cheese

TIP: You can change up the veggies and cheese in this recipe. Another favorite is spinach and feta cheese or broccoli and Cheddar. Even when changing up the other veggies, I always keep the potatoes in this dish.

WONTON-WRAPPED EGG NESTS

If you're on brunch duty, these wonton beauties definitely dress to impress. Your guests will be "foodstagramming" photos of them all over social media. Yes, they are *that* cute. They bake into crispy, golden nests that fit perfectly in the hands of little eaters and grown-ups alike. And did I mention that these little nom-noms are absolutely delicious? Try fresh spinach with creamy feta. *Yum.* You'll also fangirl over the longevity of these delightful egg nests. Bake a double batch for a weekend brunch, tuck the rest in an airtight container in the refrigerator, and you will be set to start your weekdays with a scrumptious work of culinary art.

Prep Time: 5 minutes   Cook Time: 15 minutes   Makes 12 egg nests

Preheat the oven to 375°F (191°C).

In a medium bowl, lightly whisk together the eggs and salt. Mix in the vegetables.

Coat a muffin pan with cooking spray, and press a wonton wrapper into each opening to form a cup. Then press a second wonton into the cup diagonally so all sides are covered.

Fill cups three-quarters full with egg and vegetable mixture.

Sprinkle 1 teaspoon of cheese on top of the egg mixture.

Bake uncovered until eggs are set and lightly browned on top, 13 to 15 minutes.

6 eggs, slightly beaten

½ teaspoon kosher salt

½ to ¾ cup (70 to 120 g) fresh chopped vegetables

24 wonton wrappers

¼ cup (28 g) shredded cheese of choice (I prefer sharp Cheddar)

> **TIPS:** This is one of my favorite dishes to serve at brunch. I usually only add cheese to half of the muffins in case someone does not eat dairy.
>
> You can find the wonton wrappers in the refrigerator section of most grocery stores.

KID-APPROVED HEALTHY BLUEBERRY MUFFINS

(DF, NF, SF, V)

I vividly remember when my son started playing soccer. He had teeny-tiny cleats and itty-bitty shin guards. He and his teammates would run willy-nilly across the field, sometimes toward the ball and quite often away from it. Although the kids seemed to enjoy the game, the universal highlight was digging into the weekly breakfast game treats—typically donut holes or prepackaged muffins. To my horror, my son became obsessed with a mass-produced product whose marketing included the promise that the muffins are "produced and packaged to retain their freshness up to 55 days." Momma Chef grabbed her cape and sprang into action, creating a winning recipe after multiple attempts and valuable feedback from my favorite little taste-taster. The healthy base infused with honey is the perfect platform to allow fresh blueberries to shine. This yummy treat is sure to please the pickiest player on your team—or at your table.

Prep Time: 5 minutes   Cook Time: 15 minutes   Makes 12 to 14 muffins

Preheat the oven to 375°F (191°C). Use cooking spray to coat a 12-cup muffin pan, or use paper liners.

In a large mixing bowl, add the flour, honey, eggs, baking powder and oil. Blend with a hand mixer on medium speed for about 2 minutes.

Add the blueberries to the bowl, and gently fold them into the batter.

Divide the batter among the prepared muffin pan cups.

Bake the muffins uncovered for 15 to 20 minutes until a toothpick inserted into the center comes out clean.

1½ cups (180 g) whole wheat or all-purpose flour

½ cup (120 ml) honey

2 eggs

1 teaspoon baking powder

½ cup (120 ml) avocado oil or grapeseed oil

2 cups (296 g) fresh blueberries

TIP: The muffins will stay fresh in an airtight container or zip-top bag for 2 days. After 2 days, store them in the refrigerator.

ONE-BOWL PINEAPPLE NOODLE KUGEL

(NF, SF, V)

If you grew up observing Jewish holidays, you know kugel. You're a devotee of your Bubbe's recipe, and you have a strong opinion whether kugel should be sweet or savory. If you've never had kugel before, these ingredients might give you pause: cottage cheese and noodles mixed with sugar, milk and fruit? Trust me: Momma Chef would not lead you astray.

Many years ago, I worked in an office that was big on potlucks. Although I had the date circled on my daytime planner (remember those days before smartphones?), I totally forgot about it until the night before. Fortunately, I had everything on hand to make kugel. I still remember the satisfaction of bringing home an empty casserole dish; my colleagues had scraped it clean. It was a hit!

Prep Time: 5 minutes   Cook Time: 55 minutes   Serves 8 to 10

Preheat the oven to 375°F (191°C).

In a large mixing bowl, add the eggs, cottage cheese, milk, sugar and pineapple with its juices. Using an electric mixer on low speed, blend the egg mixture until smooth, about 2 minutes.

Add the egg noodles into the mixture and stir with a spoon until everything is well combined.

Coat a 9 x 13–inch (23 x 33–cm) baking dish with cooking spray, and pour the mixture into the dish. Cover the dish tightly with aluminum foil.

Bake covered for 35 minutes, then remove the foil and bake an additional 20 minutes uncovered until the kugel is set and golden on the top. Let it cool for 15 minutes before serving.

3 eggs

1 (16-ounce [450-g]) container cottage cheese

2 cups (480 ml) whole or 2 percent milk

¾ cup (150 g) granulated sugar

1 (20-ounce [567-g]) can crushed pineapple (see Tips)

1 (12-ounce [340-g]) bag wide egg noodles

TIPS: You read the recipe right: You do not need to boil the noodles before adding them to the mixture.

If you don't like pineapple, you can substitute it with a can of sliced peaches in juice or simply omit fruit from the recipe.

As a fun addition, you can add 1 cup (75 g) of crushed corn-flakes to the top of the kugel before cooking.

THE FAMOUS BLINTZ SOUFFLÉ

(NF, SF, V)

Here, nostalgia meets comfort in the cheesy and fruity goodness of our family's famous blintz soufflé. This has long been my mother's go-to brunch recipe, and its taste and smell still evoke sweet memories of my childhood. Even though I've grown up to become Momma Chef, I've got a confession to make: I still ask my mom to bring this dish to every family brunch. I use the same recipe, but nothing tastes better to me than a dish made with my mother's love. If you have some hesitant eaters at the table, offer them a bit of powdered sugar to sprinkle on top. It's one of my tried-and-true tricks to persuade picky eaters to try something new.

Prep Time: 5 minutes   Cook Time: 45 minutes   Makes 12 blintzes

Preheat the oven to 350°F (177°C).

Coat a 9 x 13-inch (23 x 33-cm) baking dish with cooking spray, and place the blintzes seam side down in the dish.

In a large mixing bowl, add the eggs, sugar, vanilla, orange juice and sour cream. Using an electric mixer on medium speed, blend until smooth, about 2 minutes.

Pour the egg mixture over the blintzes.

Bake uncovered for 45 minutes, or until the top is golden and puffy.

12 frozen cheese blintzes (about 2 packages)

6 eggs

½ cup (100 g) granulated sugar

2 teaspoons (10 ml) vanilla extract

¼ cup (60 ml) orange juice

1 cup (240 ml) regular or low-fat sour cream (do not use fat free)

TIPS: If you prefer, you can use fruit-filled blintzes instead of cheese blintzes.

If serving this for company, I like to sprinkle the top with some powdered sugar right before serving.

HIDDEN ZUCCHINI MUFFINS

(DF, NF, SF, V)

I almost named this recipe "Magic Muffins." *Abracadabra!* You will never guess the mystery ingredient of vegetables in these muffins. (It's a cup of grated zucchini.) Presto! Add some chocolate chips, and they become a healthy dessert. You'll be everyone's favorite kitchen wizard as you mix up these treats with only one bowl (or cauldron) needed. As your final trick, these muffins will completely disappear.

Prep Time: 5 minutes   Cook Time: 15 minutes   Makes 12 to 14 muffins

Preheat the oven to 375°F (191°C). Grease a 12-muffin pan with cooking spray or use paper liners.

In a large mixing bowl, add the flour, zucchini, brown sugar, eggs, baking powder and butter.

Using a hand mixer on medium speed, blend for about 3 minutes.

Divide the batter among the prepared muffin pan cups.

Bake uncovered for 15 to 20 minutes until a toothpick inserted into the center comes out clean.

2 cups (250 g) all-purpose flour

1 cup (124 g) peeled and finely grated zucchini

1 cup (220 g) light brown sugar

3 eggs

1 teaspoon baking powder

½ cup (114 g) salted butter or margarine, melted

TIPS: You can add ½ cup (84 g) of chocolate chips to the recipe (my kids prefer semisweet).

I like to make these in colorful muffin cup liners; it's more fun for the kids!

If making these muffins dairy free, be sure to use margarine.

You can also substitute 1 banana in place of 1 cup (124 g) of grated zucchini, and see which recipe you like most!

If you like the taste of pumpkin, you can add 1 teaspoon of pumpkin pie spice to the batter.

SNACKS AND NOSHES

Allow this chapter to help you embrace entertaining without exhausting the cook. Here, you'll find easy-but-spectacular appetizers to share at home or bring to family, friends and work functions. The recipes are unbelievably delicious, but more important, their ease of preparation will allow you to be fully present for the tailgate, the family gathering and the neighborhood party. Experiment with a few and find your go-to favorites. Soon, you'll no longer have to rush to the deli department to grab a tiresome cheese-and-cracker tray to bring to your next event. In less time than it takes to make a store purchase, you can whip up delicious Easy-Peasy Hummus (page 102) or savory Black Olive and Thyme Tapenade (page 97).

Being fully present means the cook gets to watch the game. For me, that means cheering for my favorite team. Our family loves the Chicago Bears, like L.O.V.E.S. the Bears. On game days, we religiously gather around our television to cheer them to victory. Although they haven't made it to the playoffs in my youngest son's lifetime, our hope and enthusiasm never dims. Our house actually shakes when my husband and sons start jumping around, celebrating an exciting touchdown. And should our beloved navy-and-orange defense sack a Green Bay Packer, our hollering can be heard down the block. I don't want to miss a moment running back and forth to the kitchen during these family rituals. Sure, my mom-cheering and my propensity for feeling bad for the losing team may drive my kids crazy. All is forgiven, though, when we can share Three-Ingredient Chicken Wings (page 94) or The Hit of the Party: Baked Salami (page 109).

Being fully present also means that the cook can connect with people rather than being isolated in the kitchen. Because these recipes require such little prep, I can fully socialize at our summer barbecues. I can gather with friends and family around an Easy Taco Dip with Avocado Crema (page 98), Simple Baba Ganoush (page 106) or Baked Spinach-Artichoke Dip (page 101). The whole point of creating simple and delicious recipes is to build and celebrate community. These tried-and-true recipes will enhance and escalate your gatherings without sacrificing camaraderie with the people you love. Nosh away, dear friends, nosh away!

SWEET-AND-SOUR MEATBALLS

(DF, GF, NF, SF)

You'll absolutely love the versatility of this recipe. It's perfect for any occasion. You'll definitely want to serve these tasty treats at college football tailgates, NFL Sunday gatherings and Super Bowl parties. Give little hands something to do: Place the warmed meatballs on a platter, and they can skewer them with fun football-themed toothpicks. My friend loves to make a Crock-Pot full of these sweet-and-sour delicacies for an easy and tasty dinner on cool fall nights. Her kids love them over rice or mixed with a little whole wheat pasta. No matter the occasion, anyone who enjoys them always asks for more.

Prep Time: 5 minutes   Cook Time: 25 minutes   Makes 20 meatballs

In a large mixing bowl, mix the beef, egg and breadcrumbs until well combined, and shape the mixture into 20 golf ball–sized meatballs.

In a medium pot, add the jelly and chili sauce, and cook over medium-high heat for about 3 minutes, mixing constantly with a wooden spoon to combine.

If you are making this on the stove, add the meatballs to the pot, and gently stir to make sure they are covered in the sauce. Reduce the heat to low, cover the pot, and cook covered for about 25 minutes, until the meatballs are cooked through.

If you are making this in a slow cooker, add the cooked sauce to the bottom of the slow cooker, and place the meatballs on top of the sauce. Cook on high for 2 to 3 hours until the meatballs are cooked through.

1 pound (454 g) ground beef (at least 90 percent lean)

1 egg

½ cup (28 g) unseasoned breadcrumbs (regular or gluten free)

1 cup (240 ml) grape jelly (see Tips)

1 cup (240 ml) chili sauce (see Tips)

TIPS: I like to use Heinz Chili Sauce in this recipe because other chili sauce brands can be spicy.

If you don't have grape jelly on hand, you can use strawberry jelly.

In a pinch, you can use premade frozen meatballs. Just follow the directions above when adding the meatballs to the sauce; you will only need to cook these for 15 to 20 minutes.

THREE-INGREDIENT CHICKEN WINGS

(DF, EF, GF, NF, SF)

Life is really simple, but we insist on making it complicated.
—Confucius

Was Confucius discussing my chicken wing recipe when he extolled simplicity? Who's to say? This recipe definitely embraces his ancient words of wisdom: Why complicate simple perfection? With just three ingredients, you, too, will be blown away by this scrumptious appetizer.

If one of my son's friends samples these wings for the first time at our house, nine times out of ten, I'm going to get a call requesting the recipe. Hands down it's my most popular dish and an absolute favorite of kids and adults alike. No football gathering is complete without these addictively tangy wings. I learned the hard way that I must make a separate tray for the kids; otherwise, my sons and their friends would never leave any for the adults. This appetizer easily transforms into a main dish as a family-favorite dinner.

Prep Time: 5 minutes   Cook Time: 30 minutes   Serves 8

Preheat the oven to 375°F (191°C).

In a small bowl, mix the soy sauce and barbecue sauce.

On a large baking sheet, spread the chicken wings in a single layer.

Pour the sauce over the chicken wings, making sure the sauce covers all the wings.

Bake the wings uncovered for 30 minutes, then turn your oven to broil, and broil the wings for about 3 minutes to crisp them on top. Make sure to watch them while they broil so they do not burn.

2 tablespoons (30 ml) soy sauce, regular or gluten free

½ cup (120 ml) barbecue sauce

2 pounds (907 g) chicken wings (see Tips)

TIPS: For this recipe, I like to use a large aluminum disposable pan because the sauce can stick to the baking sheet, making it hard to clean.

You can substitute the wings for chicken drumettes, which little kids may prefer as they are easier to hold.

BLACK OLIVE AND THYME TAPENADE

(DF, GF, LC, NF, SF, V)

One reason I love this recipe is because of how happy it makes my family. This tapenade was inspired by my family's olive obsession. My husband and all three of our boys can't get enough of them. In fact, they name olives as their favorite "vegetable."

Tapenade is typically found on the fancy shelves at the grocery stores. After years of purchasing jar after jar, I finally decided the time had come to see if I could make it on my own. The answer was a resounding yes. It takes a mere 5 minutes to make this savory spread, and less than 24 hours for my family to devour it. Serve it with pita chips, spoon it over chicken or spread it on crusty French bread. If you prefer to eat it by the spoonful, I'll never tell.

Prep Time: 5 minutes   Serves 4

In a food processor, combine the olive oil, olives, lemon juice, garlic, thyme and mayonnaise, if using. Pulse until the mixture becomes a coarse paste (stopping twice during the blending to scrape down the sides of the bowl).

Taste the tapenade, and add salt to taste, if needed.

> **TIPS:** This can be made with pitted green olives in place of the black olives.
>
> If you like a little kick, add a small dash of red pepper flakes before pulsing the mixture.

¼ cup (60 ml) extra-virgin olive oil

1 cup (180 g) black olives, pitted (see Tips)

1 tablespoon (15 ml) lemon juice

2 small cloves garlic

1 teaspoon chopped fresh thyme

2 teaspoons (10 ml) mayonnaise, optional

EASY TACO DIP WITH AVOCADO CREMA

(EF, GF, NF, SF, V)

When it comes to noshing, chips and taco dip are must-haves—and don't be surprised at how many people *must have* this recipe from you! The avocado layer elevates this easy taco dip to the next level of party-food perfection. (Be forewarned, though: once you try this recipe, you'll no longer be satisfied by the premade layered dips in your grocery's deli section.) You'll especially love that this version spends a few minutes in the oven, melting the cheese layers into a beautiful blend that can best be described as a fiesta in your mouth. Don't try and mix the cream cheese mixture by hand; use a hand mixer to make the mixture lighter and easier to spread. This dip pairs best with hearty corn tortilla chips such as El Ranchero. A pitcher of margaritas wouldn't hurt either.

Prep Time: 5 minutes   Cook Time: 10 minutes   Serves 4

Preheat the oven to 375°F (191°C).

Spread the refried beans in a 9 x 13–inch (23 x 33–cm) baking dish.

In a large mixing bowl, add the avocados, cream cheese and taco seasoning.

Using a hand mixer on medium speed, blend the avocado mixture for 2 minutes until well combined. Add the olives, and gently stir with a spoon to mix everything together.

Spread the avocado mixture over the beans.

Top with the cheese, and bake uncovered for 10 minutes.

TIP: If you want to add meat to this recipe, brown 1 pound (454 g) of ground beef, and use it in place of the refried beans. If swapping out the beans for ground beef, this becomes a low-carb recipe.

1 (16-ounce [453-g]) can vegetarian refried beans

2 very ripe avocados, skin and pits removed

1 (8-ounce [232-g]) package cream cheese, softened

2 tablespoons (28 g) taco seasoning, regular or gluten free

1 (4.25-ounce [120-g]) can chopped black olives, drained

1 cup (113 g) shredded Cheddar cheese

BAKED SPINACH-ARTICHOKE DIP

(GF, LC, NF, SF, V)

You can't go wrong with this decadent and delicious crowd-pleaser. Just a whiff of this recipe, and I'm back in college, where my friends and I are treating ourselves to a sit-down restaurant, splurging on a bubbling crock of baked spinach-artichoke dip. Our midterm worries would melt away as we dipped crunchy cracker after crunchy cracker into our favorite comfort food. Years later, this iconic dish still delivers. It's the yummiest of respites from everyday stress. Don't fool yourself into thinking you'll have leftovers of this dish. Once it's out of the oven, this dip disappears in no time.

Prep Time: 5 minutes   Cook Time: 25 minutes   Serves 6

Preheat the oven to 375°F (191°C).

In a mixing bowl, stir together the spinach, mayonnaise, artichokes, sour cream, soup mix and Parmesan.

Coat a 9 x 13–inch (23 x 33–cm) baking dish with cooking spray, and spread the spinach-artichoke mixture evenly into the dish.

Bake uncovered for 25 minutes.

> **TIPS:** I like to serve this warm with pita chips or tortilla chips.
>
> You can make this dish in advance. When you're ready to serve it, remove the dish from the refrigerator, cover the dish with aluminum foil, and bake at 300°F (149°C) for 10 minutes or until warm.

1 (10-ounce [283-g]) package frozen spinach, thawed and well drained

¼ cup (60 ml) mayonnaise

1 (14-ounce [397-g]) can quartered artichokes, well drained

1 cup (240 ml) sour cream

1 (1-ounce [27-g]) envelope dry vegetable soup mix, regular or gluten free

½ cup (50 g) shredded Parmesan cheese

EASY-PEASY HUMMUS

(DF, EG, GF, NF, V)

In the words of Queen Beyoncé: *Who run the world? Girls.*

Nowhere is this powerful sisterhood better illustrated than in hair salons. Hairdressers and customers share secrets, struggles and recipes. Years ago, my hairdresser changed my life with her amazing hummus recipe. Not only did she tell me about her mind-blowing hummus, she followed up by bringing me a container at my next appointment. Was my mind blown? I'm not going to lie: It was absolutely spectacular. My husband and I agreed it was the best hummus we'd ever eaten (and we've eaten a lot of hummus!). Thanks to Linda for graciously sharing her recipe, which I slightly tweaked based on the spices on my shelf. You'll want to stock up on cans of chickpeas, so you'll always be prepared to make a batch to bring to your next gathering.

Prep Time: 5 minutes   Serves 6

In a food processor or blender, add the chickpeas and the liquid from 1 can of the chickpeas, the olive oil, lemon juice, tahini, garlic and seasoning salt.

Puree until smooth and well combined, about 2 minutes.

2 (15.5-ounce [439-g]) cans chickpeas, drained (reserve liquid from 1 can)

½ cup (120 ml) extra-virgin olive oil

Juice of 1 lemon

½ cup (120 ml) tahini

3 cloves garlic

1 teaspoon seasoning salt

> **TIPS:** If serving this to guests, I like to sprinkle the hummus with a dash of paprika.
>
> This can be stored in an airtight container in the refrigerator for up to 5 days.
>
> This recipe is nut free, but it is not sesame free as the tahini contains sesame.
>
> In most grocery stores, you can find tahini in the international food aisle (I get mine there) or in the condiment aisle near the peanut butter.

SAVORY CHEESE BOUREKAS

(NF, SF, V)

You may have not heard of bourekas before, but—I promise—in one form or another, you've at the very least sampled one of its cousins. Calzones, empanadas, strudel, samosas and bourekas—they are all based on the fundamental truth that everything tastes better when it's wrapped in pastry.

Look no further than this recipe to carry on the tradition of these flaky pockets of flavor. Serve them at baby showers, happy hour, book club—or whenever you're craving some cheesy goodness swaddled in layers of crispy, buttery delight.

Prep Time: 5 minutes   Cook Time: 20 minutes   Makes 9 bourekas

Preheat the oven to 375°F (191°C). Spray a baking sheet with cooking spray, or line it with parchment paper.

In a medium bowl, add the feta, ricotta, mozzarella and egg, and mix until well combined.

Cut the puff pastry into 9 equal-sized squares, and add 1 tablespoon (14 g) of the cheese mixture into the center of each of the squares.

Add water into a small bowl and, using your finger, lightly rub water around the edges of the puff pastry; this helps it seal.

Take one corner of the puff pastry, and fold it diagonally to the other corner, so it forms a triangle. Press firmly around the edges to seal the triangle.

Place the triangles on the prepared baking sheet.

Bake uncovered for 20 to 25 minutes until the bourekas have puffed up and are golden brown.

½ cup (75 g) crumbled feta cheese

¼ cup (62 g) ricotta cheese

¼ cup (28 g) shredded mozzarella cheese

1 egg, lightly beaten

1 sheet puff pastry, defrosted

TIPS: Occasionally, I can find precut puff pastry squares in the freezer section of some grocery stores. If you are lucky to find these, grab them and skip the step of cutting the pastry into squares.

You can add toppings to the bourekas before you cook them. Just brush the tops with some lightly beaten egg, and sprinkle on some sesame seeds, poppy seeds or, my favorite, everything bagel seasoning.

SIMPLE BABA GANOUSH

(DF, GF, LC, NF, SF, V)

Baba ganoush is a simply delicious dip to prepare: a smooth and nutrient-rich alternative to the ever-popular hummus. I've made it so often through the years that I no longer use measurements or directions; I'm just on autopilot. I had to dig back through the years and reach out to my friends to find the specifications of my original recipe. Fortunately, it's been requested so often that it didn't take long to find a copy. In the unlikely event that you have leftovers, you can make a delicious lunch the next day: spread it on a pita stuffed with your favorite fresh veggies. Yum!

Prep Time: 5 minutes   Cook Time: 50 minutes   Serves 6 to 8

Preheat the oven to 450°F (232°C), and adjust a rack to the upper third of the oven.

Place the eggplant on an aluminum foil–lined baking sheet and, using a fork, prick the eggplant in several places.

Bake the eggplant for about 25 minutes on each side until it is very soft.

In a large mixing bowl, combine the mayonnaise, olive oil, garlic, lemon juice and salt.

Remove the eggplant from the oven, split it down the middle, and scrape out the flesh.

Add the eggplant flesh to the mayonnaise mixture, and stir well.

Cover and refrigerate for at least 2 hours before serving to let flavors blend together.

1 large eggplant

2 tablespoons (30 ml) mayonnaise

2 tablespoons (30 ml) extra-virgin olive oil

2 cloves garlic, chopped

2 tablespoons (30 ml) lemon juice

½ teaspoon kosher salt

TIPS: Before serving this to guests, I like to sprinkle the baba ganoush with some fresh parsley or paprika.

This baba ganoush will stay good in an airtight container in the refrigerator for up to 5 days.

THE HIT OF THE PARTY: BAKED SALAMI

(DF, EF, GF, NF, SF)

This recipe will be the hero of your appetizer table. The intensity of the mustard, the sweetness of the jam and the salty goodness of the salami create a tantalizing treat for your taste buds. If you're serving this for a larger crowd, I suggest making two salamis. You'll see how fast they go! Let the record show that I almost single-handedly devoured this ambrosial concoction the first time I had it at a friend's house. She intervened—perhaps in fear that I would lick the plate clean—and kindly shared this legendary recipe with me.

If you've never bought a whole salami before, don't fret. They are available in every major grocery store; just ask someone in the deli department to help you find them.

Prep Time: 5 minutes   Cook Time: 40 minutes   Serves 8 as an appetizer

Preheat the oven to 350°F (177°C).

Score the salami into ¼-inch (6-mm)-thick slices, making sure the slices do not go all the way through.

Place the salami into an 8 x 8-inch (20 x 20–cm) baking dish or aluminum pan.

In a small bowl, mix the mustard and jam until well combined. Spread half of the mustard mixture all over the scored salami. Save the rest of the mixture to serve on the side as a dipping sauce.

Wrap the salami in foil and bake for 35 minutes, then uncover the salami and bake for an additional 10 minutes.

1 (2-pound [907-g]) whole soft salami

1 (8-ounce [240-ml]) jar Dijon mustard, such as Grey Poupon

1 (12-ounce [355-ml]) jar apricot jam

TIPS: Do not use a hard or dry salami; it will be hard to cut. If you cannot find a 2-pound (907-g) salami, you can use a 1-pound (454-g) piece and make two of them.

You can serve the salami as is, or cut it into small squares and serve it with toothpicks.

HOT CRAB MEAT DIP

(LC, NF, SF)

When I was growing up, my mom made this classic and addictive hot dip whenever she hosted dinner parties. As a picky eater and opinionated child, I would not even try a single bite: There was no way I was going to eat crab. In a plot twist that surprised no one, when I grew up, I had to admit—once again—that mother knows best. I regret that I ever rejected this luxurious, creamy delight. Fortunately, my oldest son was born with a more sophisticated palate, and he has loved this dip his entire life. Now that he's a teenager with a voracious adolescent appetite, he easily accounts for three of the six servings per batch. In this recipe, "hot" refers to the temperature and not the spicy factor, although a shake or two of hot sauce will add a little heat.

Prep Time: 5 minutes   Cook Time: 20 minutes   Serves 6

Preheat the oven to 375°F (191°C).

In a large bowl, place the cream cheese, mayonnaise, sour cream and Old Bay seasoning, and with an electric mixer on low speed, blend until smooth, about 2 minutes.

Add the crab meat, and blend on low speed for another minute until the crab meat is shredded into the mixture and everything is well combined.

Coat an 8 x 8-inch (20 x 20-cm) baking dish with cooking spray, and spread the mixture evenly into the dish.

Sprinkle the top with the shredded Parmesan cheese, and bake uncovered for 20 to 25 minutes until the top is golden brown.

1 (8-ounce [232-g]) package cream cheese, softened

¼ cup (60 ml) mayonnaise

⅓ cup (80 ml) sour cream

1 teaspoon Old Bay seasoning

12 to 15 ounces (339 to 426 g) imitation crab meat, flake style (see Tips)

½ cup (50 g) shredded Parmesan cheese

TIPS: In place of imitation crab meat, you can use 1 pound (454 g) of chopped lump crab meat.

You can find Old Bay seasoning at any grocery store in the spice aisle. I have even seen it at Target and Walmart.

SRIRACHA-HONEY WINGS

(DF, EF, GF, NF, SF)

Momma Chef Food Lesson: If you mentioned sriracha before 2010, most people would have responded with a blank stare. It was a secret among a small group of chefs and hipsters. Fast forward a decade, and sriracha-flavored products now flood the market. Although there are plenty of knock-off sauces, I swear by the original bottled by Huy Fong. In the supermarket, look for a plastic bottle containing a vibrant red sauce, topped with a bright green lid.

The honey in the recipe provides a sweet contrast to the sriracha. The teaspoon will only spice it up a bit. My family prefers a bit more heat, so I double the amount of sriracha. You'll make this so often that you'll want to bookmark this page—although the tell-tale sriracha stains from your fingers on the pages may take care of that for you.

Prep Time: 5 minutes   Cook Time: 30 minutes   Serves 8

Preheat the oven to 400°F (204°C).

In a small bowl, mix the sriracha, paprika, soy sauce and honey.

On a large baking sheet, spread the chicken wings out in a single layer.

Pour the sauce over the chicken wings, making sure the sauce covers all the wings.

Bake the wings uncovered for 30 minutes, flipping them over halfway through.

Turn your oven to broil, and broil the wings for just about 3 minutes to crisp them on top. Make sure to watch them while they broil so they do not burn.

1 teaspoon sriracha

½ teaspoon smoked paprika

½ cup (120 ml) soy sauce, regular or gluten free

½ cup (120 ml) honey

2 pounds (907 g) chicken wings

> **TIP:** For this recipe, I always use a large, aluminum disposable pan because the sauce can stick to the pan, making it hard to clean.

BUILD YOUR BOWL

I love living in a four-season state. For this chapter, it was my delight to pull together recipes to reflect the seasonal contrasts of salads and soups.

Summer is by far my favorite season. Vitamin D, family time and summer camp! I love sitting on our patio, hosting barbecues and eating ice cream. My kids and I can hang out instead of battling over homework versus screen time. I cannot wait for June every year. Oh, and my fresh summer tomatoes shine in a Tuscan-inspired bread salad to die for—Panzanella Salad with Herbs and Mozzarella (page 130).

Except, when September rolls around, I realize that fall is *really* my favorite season. The weather cools down, and I can wear a comfy flannel shirt to watch my sons play soccer rather than melting on a 98-degree July day. Every fall is made better with every rich and creamy bowl of Autumn Butternut Squash Soup (page 126). The brilliantly colored leaves, the Chicago Bears, pumpkin pie—you name it, fall is hands down the best.

But in December, I remember that winter *truly* tops my favorite season list. The festivities, the gift-giving, the family gatherings! For a winter holiday party, I love to serve the festive Beautiful Fresh Beet and Burrata Salad (page 129). The cold temperatures light the fire of my creative juices, and my recipe writing kicks into high gear. To warm up our bones on a freezing January night, I'll be sure to have Mom's Original Chicken Noodle Soup (page 117) on the back burner, simmering. Winter can't be beat.

It's just that when spring arrives in Chicago, it's 100 percent for sure my favorite season. At last, the gray residue of the last big snowfall has melted. Little purple flowers peek out of the ground. The smell of fresh rain? Euphoric. Spring symbolizes hope and new beginnings. When the ice melts and spring is sprung, we like to celebrate with something on the grill, paired with the Colorful Coleslaw and Ramen Salad (page 133). I'd be crazy not to name spring as the best season ever.

In this chapter, you'll find a selection of my family's favorites. In the tradition of "Pick Two" combinations, look to pair these comforting soups with crisp salads. While many of the recipes can stand alone, no one's going to stop you from adding a crusty loaf of bread or a simple sandwich to round out a meal.

MOM'S ORIGINAL CHICKEN NOODLE SOUP

(DF, GF, NF, SF)

Get ready: I'm about to change the life of you and your family. For real. Here it is: my "You-absolutely-must-not-miss-this-under-any-circumstances" recipe. This miraculous chicken soup's powers range from soothing sore throats to easing heartaches. Plus, it's chock-full of simple goodness. During the 2020 pandemic quarantine, I was making this comfort food for my family by the gallon. Each bowl sustained us both physically and somehow emotionally—its elixir properties strengthened us to face each day's uncertainties in those "unprecedented times" (may we never hear that phrase again). Upon preparing my third batch (Or maybe the fifth? Or the eighth? It's a bit of a blur) of quarantine soup, I had an epiphany: I could skip the step of boiling the noodles separately—they could cook right in the soup! I love finding ways to save time. Gluten free? Skip the noodles, *but for the love of all good things*—don't skip the soup. You could always substitute gluten-free noodles as well.

Prep Time: 5 minutes   Cook Time: 45 minutes   Serves 6

In a large soup pot, add the chicken, chicken broth, carrots, celery and dill. Cook over medium-high heat until the soup is boiling, about 5 minutes.

Cover the pot, and reduce the heat to low.

Simmer the soup covered for 25 minutes, stirring occasionally.

Add the egg noodles, and cook uncovered on low heat for another 20 minutes, stirring occasionally.

Season with salt as needed.

1 pound (454 g) boneless, skinless chicken thighs or breasts, cut into strips

2 (32-ounce [960-ml]) boxes chicken broth

2 large carrots, peeled and cut into chunks

3 celery ribs, leaves removed, cut into chunks

1 tablespoon (3 g) finely chopped fresh dill

1 cup (227 g) uncooked wide egg noodles

CREAMY CAULIFLOWER SOUP

(EF, GF, LC, NF, SF, V)

You're a pretty great person. My evidence? You're reading a recipe about cauliflower soup! If you're debating whether or not to make this soup for dinner, *make it*. Let me assure you that you will have made a good decision. We both know it's all about trial and error as we navigate the best ways to take care of our kids, our partners and ourselves. I've already done the trial and error for you to create this creamy dish. The result is that all four of my boys (three sons, one husband) love, love, love this soup. They can demolish crocks of it like an NFL football team. I'm sure your family will be no different. Plus, this recipe provides another clever way to sneak some extra veggies into your family's diet.

Prep Time: 5 minutes   Cook Time: 40 minutes   Serves 8

In a large soup pot, heat the olive oil over medium heat, and sauté the onion for 3 minutes.

Add the vegetable broth, cauliflower and celery root, and stir to combine.

Partially cover the pot, and cook for 40 minutes until the cauliflower is very tender.

Remove from the heat, and puree the soup in a blender, food processor or using an immersion blender until smooth.

Mix in the heavy cream and salt to taste.

¼ cup (60 ml) extra-virgin olive oil

1 medium yellow onion, chopped

5 cups (1.2 L) vegetable broth

2 (10- to 12-ounce [125- to 160-g]) bags cauliflower florets

2 cups (312 g) celery root, peeled and diced

¼ cup (60 ml) heavy cream (see Tips)

> **TIPS:** To make this dairy free, omit the heavy cream or use coconut milk.
>
> When serving the soup, you can garnish it with chopped chives, chopped parsley or, my favorite, small croutons.

VEGETARIAN SPLIT PEA SOUP WITH DILL

(DF, EG, GF, NF, SF, V)

This is my dad's favorite soup, and I love making it for him. He requests it for any and all occasions. After surgery, people sent him get-well cards and flowers. To me, he said, "Please bring over the soup." Pulled tooth? "Karen, please bring over the soup." Whenever I ask him how I can help on any given day, the answer is always "make the soup." Listen to my dad—*make the soup.*

To keep the veggies "hidden" from the suspicious eyes of any anti-vegetarians, don't forget to puree your final product. Invest in an immersion blender to avoid the hassle and mess of transferring your soup to a blender. Friend to friend, let me offer you a tried-and-true way to convince my little eaters to try new soups: give them a separate small bowl of tiny croutons to sprinkle on top. I'm not sure why adding their own toppings makes food more appealing to kids, but it works over here every time!

Prep Time: 5 minutes   Cook Time: 45 minutes   Serves 6

In a large soup pot, heat the olive oil over medium heat, and sauté the onion for 3 minutes.

Add the split peas and carrots, and cook for another 2 minutes.

Add the vegetable broth and dill, and stir to combine.

Partially cover the pot, and cook for 45 minutes until the peas are very tender.

Remove from the heat, and puree the soup in batches in a blender, food processor or with an immersion blender until smooth.

2 tablespoons (30 ml) extra-virgin olive oil

1 medium yellow onion, chopped

1 cup (225 g) dry green split peas

1 (8-ounce [226-g]) bag baby carrots

6 cups (1.4 L) vegetable broth

1 teaspoon dried dill

CREAMY CARROT AND SWEET POTATO SOUP

(DF, EF, GF, NF, SF, V)

Fortunately, for most of us living with picky-vegetable eaters, carrots tend to be universally loved. At any given time of day (or night), the odds are that someone in my house will be munching on carrots—and, yes, straight out of the bag. This recipe morphs my family's favorite snacking veggie into creamy bowls of deliciousness. In addition to its great taste, there are nearly a bazillion other reasons to be over-the-moon about this recipe. For starters, carrots are so ridiculously healthy—chock-full of antioxidants and vitamins. Plus, you know I'm a sucker for lovely things, and this soup is drop-dead gorgeous—a vibrant orange that will cheer you up on a gray November day or promise spring on a chilly February night. Seriously, I could yammer on and on about why I love this recipe, but a bowl is worth a thousand words.

Prep Time: 5 minutes   Cook Time: 55 minutes   Serves 8

In a large soup pot, heat the olive oil over medium heat, and sauté the onion for 3 minutes.

Add the carrots, sweet potatoes, vegetable broth and thyme, and mix well.

Partially cover the pot, reduce the heat to medium-low and cook for 55 minutes until the carrots and sweet potatoes are very tender.

Remove from the heat, and puree the soup in batches in a blender, food processor or with an immersion blender until smooth.

TIP: I always buy the sweet potatoes and onions already precut; you can find these in the vegetable refrigerated section at most grocery stores.

2 tablespoons (30 ml) extra-virgin olive oil

1 cup (160 g) diced white or yellow onion

1 (16-ounce [452-g]) bag baby carrots

2 cups (268 g) sweet potatoes, peeled and diced (about 2 medium sweet potatoes)

2 (32-ounce [960-ml]) boxes vegetable broth

2 teaspoons (2 g) dried thyme

YEMENITE CHICKEN AND VEGETABLE SOUP

(DF, EF, GF, LC, NF, SF)

This delicious soup is all about a mystery spice—hawaij (pronounced "hu-why-adge"). *Hawaij*, which means "mixture" in Arabic, is a warm blend of cumin, coriander, turmeric, black pepper and cardamom.

After tasting this deliciously distinctive soup, my son said, "I can't place the taste, but it's so unique and it's *so good*." Case in point: he circled back to this recipe the following week. He made a batch on his own, ramping it up with his own personal flair by adding in a package of ramen noodles (minus the seasoning packet). I was beaming with pride: The apprentice of hawaij-seasoned soup became the master!

Please note that if you order hawaij online or find it in a gourmet store, there is both a savory and sweet version. The sweeter mixture is often called "hawaij for coffee"—it's used for winter drinks and baking. Be sure to get the one for soups.

Prep Time: 5 minutes   Cook Time: 45 minutes   Serves 8

In a medium soup pot, heat the oil over medium heat, and add the chicken. Cook for 8 minutes, stirring occasionally.

Add the tomato juice, mixed vegetables, chicken broth and hawaij, and bring the soup to a boil.

Partially cover the pot, and reduce the heat to medium-low.

Cook for 35 minutes.

Remove from the heat, and add salt as needed.

> **TIP:** Hawaij spice does have a unique light yellow color, so if you have eaters who might not try the soup because of the color, you can use 1 teaspoon of seasoning salt in place of the hawaij spice.

1 tablespoon (15 ml) extra-virgin olive oil

1 pound (454 g) boneless, skinless chicken thighs, cut into 1-inch (2.5-cm) cubes

1½ cups (360 ml) tomato juice

1 (10- to 12-ounce [283- to 340-g]) bag frozen mixed vegetables, including corn, carrots and peas

1 (32-ounce [960-ml]) box chicken broth

1½ teaspoons (3 g) hawaij spice (see Tip)

AUTUMN BUTTERNUT SQUASH SOUP

(EF, GF, NF, SF, V)

Fall hasn't truly arrived until my family and I have enjoyed our first bowls of butternut squash soup. That's right. That's what I said: *squash soup*. Friends, don't roll your eyes and turn the page. Put down that pumpkin-spiced latte and give yourself 5 minutes to make this unbelievably easy-to-prepare soup. Both you and your family will be so thankful that you did. The "hardest" steps in this recipe aren't hard at all: 1) Thanks to Costco, Trader Joe's and probably your local grocery, there's precut squash. Check! 2) You have to cut an onion. Easy! 3) You have to puree batches of the prepared soup in a blender. No problem! And do you know who likes to push buttons on blenders? Kids! Make them part of the process, and they'll already be sold on tasting the creation they helped to make. Truly, the most difficult step of all will be waiting to try your first delicious spoonful.

Prep Time: 5 minutes   Cook Time: 45 minutes   Serves 8

In a large saucepan, heat the olive oil over medium heat, and sauté the onion for 3 minutes.

Add the butternut squash, mix, and cook for 2 minutes more.

Pour in the vegetable broth and 2 cups (480 ml) of water.

Partially cover the pot, and cook for 45 minutes until the butternut squash is very tender.

Remove from the heat, add in the cream cheese and brown sugar, and puree in batches in a blender, food processor or with an immersion blender until smooth.

1 tablespoon (15 ml) extra-virgin olive oil

1 small yellow onion, chopped

4 cups (464 g) cubed butternut squash

1 box (32-ounce [960-ml]) vegetable broth

1 (8-ounce [232-g]) package low-fat cream cheese

⅓ cup (73 g) light brown sugar

TIPS: Before serving, I like to sprinkle the soup with cinnamon and chopped pecans (first making sure there are no nut allergies).

I use cream cheese to give the soup a rich texture. But if you want to make it dairy free, you can put in ½ cup (120 ml) of your favorite dairy-free milk.

BEAUTIFUL FRESH BEET AND BURRATA SALAD

(EF, GF, LC, NF, SF, V)

To my absolute delight, I recently discovered burrata cheese. The process of making burrata starts out in the same way as making mozzarella; the crucial difference is that cream is added in the final step. This bit of cheese wizardry means that when you slice into burrata, rich, velvety goodness oozes out. Pure bliss.

In lieu of standing at your counter, eating bite after bite of straight burrata—which could totally happen, I'm just saying—update your recipes with this creamy nectar of the gods. It pairs beautifully with produce, inspiring me to create this salad. Here, the crunch of fresh beets contrasts perfectly with the tender burrata, while the arugula adds a peppery punch. Serve this gorgeous salad to company as it not only tastes amazing, but it also plates like a fashion queen.

Prep Time: 5 minutes   Serves 4

Spread the arugula on a serving platter.

Arrange the beets and burrata cheese on top of the arugula.

Sprinkle salt over the arugula, cheese and beets.

Drizzle the balsamic glaze over the entire dish.

1 (5-ounce [142-g]) container baby arugula

10 small cooked beets, quartered

8 ounces (226 g) burrata cheese, cut into 1-inch (2.5-cm) pieces (see Tips)

1 teaspoon kosher salt

3 tablespoons (45 ml) balsamic glaze

TIPS: If you can't find burrata, you can use buffalo mozzarella.

I like to use organic Love Beets. I can usually find these at Costco or Whole Foods.

If there are no nut allergies, you can sprinkle chopped walnuts, almonds or pistachios on the salad.

Look for the balsamic glaze in the aisle with balsamic vinegar and oils. It's similar to a salad dressing, but it has a slightly thicker consistency.

PANZANELLA SALAD WITH HERBS AND MOZZARELLA

(NF, SF, V)

Dear Panzanella,
You had me at bread!
Love, Karen

Panzanella derives from the Latin words for "bread" and "little basket." I love that someone, somewhere—probably in the Tuscan region of Italy—turned to a friend and said, "You know what the salad world needs? Fewer vegetables, more bread."

Picture this recipe as a deconstructed fresh tomato-mozzarella sandwich in a bowl; it's an absolutely *bueno* way to enjoy an abundance of summer-fresh tomatoes. The bright red tomatoes and green basil look stunning served on a brightly painted Tuscan serving dish. You can pick one up at a thrift shop or at HomeGoods.

Prep Time: 5 minutes   Cook Time: 10 minutes   Serves 6

Preheat the oven to 450°F (232°C).

In a gallon-sized zip-top bag, toss the baguette cubes with the olive oil until the bread is coated.

Lay out the bread on an aluminum foil–lined baking sheet, and bake uncovered for 10 minutes until the bread is toasted.

In a large salad bowl or large platter, add the toasted bread, mozzarella, tomatoes, basil and onion.

You can dress this salad with ½ cup (120 ml) of your favorite lemon-herb dressing. You should let the salad sit with the dressing for 30 minutes before serving so the flavors soak into the bread.

1 long baguette, cut into 1-inch (2.5-cm) cubes (3 to 4 cups [240 to 272 g])

3 tablespoons (45 ml) extra-virgin olive oil

¾ cup (169 g) fresh mozzarella, cubed

3 large tomatoes, cut into bite-sized pieces

⅓ cup (6 g) fresh basil, thinly sliced

¼ cup (40 g) sliced red onion

COLORFUL COLESLAW AND RAMEN SALAD

(DF, EG, NF, SF, V)

Make this your signature dish to bring to family gatherings, potlucks and team parties. I promise that your serving bowl will come home each and every time without a single bite left. Ramen noodles add an unexpected twist to the coleslaw, making this dish a memorable talking point for first-timers. This recipe will quickly garner legions of fans—double the recipe and you'll be the hero of every event. You can make this with plain green cabbage, but using a mix with red cabbage and carrots provides a color pop to give it visual appeal as well as taste. My family likes the added crunch of chopped cashews; you could serve them on the side to accommodate nut allergies.

Prep Time: 5 minutes   Cook Time: 5 minutes   Serves 6

In a small pot, bring 2 cups (480 ml) of water to a boil, and add the ramen noodles, keeping the seasoning packet on the side. Let the ramen noodles cook for 2 to 3 minutes until soft. Drain the noodles, and let them cool.

Meanwhile, make the dressing. In a small bowl, add the packet of chicken seasoning, olive oil, honey and rice vinegar, mixing well until everything is combined.

In a large salad bowl, add the noodles, coleslaw, green onion and dressing. Mix well.

> **TIPS:** If there are no nut allergies, you can add in ¼ cup (32 g) of chopped cashews.
>
> Make sure when you purchase the ramen, it has the flavor packet separate, not already mixed into the noodles. Usually, the flat rectangular packages have the packets separate. Do not purchase ramen in the bowls; those usually have the seasoning mixed in with the noodles.

1 (3-ounce [85-g]) package chicken-flavored ramen soup

2 tablespoons (30 ml) extra-virgin olive oil

¼ cup (60 ml) honey

2 tablespoons (30 ml) rice vinegar

1 (14-ounce [397-g]) bag three-colored coleslaw, including green cabbage, red cabbage and carrots

¼ cup (12 g) thinly sliced green onion

CAULIFLOWER SALAD WITH POMEGRANATE AND TOASTED ALMONDS

(DF, EF, GF, LC, SF, V)

The summer of 2021 found me in a low-carb phase. One afternoon, I was staring into my refrigerator, willing a low-carb treat to appear. In what can only be described as divine culinary intervention, the items on the shelves magically aligned in my brain, and this remarkable concoction was born. It's a medley of crunchy almonds, tart pomegranate, fresh mint and smooth cucumber combined with a zesty vinaigrette and a base of carb-friendly cauliflower rice. The flavors and textures blend together to create a low-carb party of delicious with a capital D. Best of all, you can throw it together in 5 minutes to quickly stave off any poor eating choices you were tempted to make. I became so obsessed with this dish that I made it at least once a week for months! If you don't have fresh mint, it's super easy to grow. Nothing beats going outside to pick a few handfuls of its fragrant leaves for this recipe (and a pitcher of mojitos!).

Prep Time: 5 minutes   Serves 6

On an aluminum foil–lined toaster-sized baking sheet, lay the almonds in a single layer. Put the baking sheet in the toaster oven, and toast for only 1 minute, keeping an eye on the almonds to make sure they are not burning.

In a large salad bowl, combine the toasted almonds, cauliflower rice, pomegranate seeds, mint, cucumber and vinaigrette, and mix well.

This can be served immediately or stored in an airtight container for up to 2 days in the refrigerator.

> **TIPS:** You need to use fresh raw cauliflower rice in this recipe; you can find it in the refrigerated section near the vegetables in most grocery stores.
>
> If you cannot find fresh cauliflower rice, it is rather easy to make. Purchase two bags of cauliflower florets, and using the food processor with the grater attachment, pulse the cauli-flower until it looks like rice.

¼ cup (27 g) slivered almonds

2 cups (114 g) fresh raw cauliflower rice

2 tablespoons (56 g) fresh pomegranate seeds

¼ cup (23 g) fresh mint, finely chopped

½ cup (52 g) diced cucumber

¼ cup (60 ml) lemon-herb vinaigrette, such as Marzetti Simply Dressed Lemon Vinaigrette

IN LIVING COLOR

Food is my love language. If you're at my table, I'm going to take care of you. And by you, I mean *everyone*. On any given night, however, I may not be 100 percent sure who exactly is going to show up at my table:

Maybe my son will ask a friend to stay for dinner.

Maybe an extended family member will bring a date to a birthday meal.

Maybe an unplanned team barbecue will organically emerge after a soccer game.

And while "the more the merrier" is my mantra, the one fear that can stress me out is making sure everyone can find something satisfying that they can and will eat. With the increasing number of people choosing a nonmeat lifestyle due to health or ethics, I learned I needed more than my go-to meatballs and chicken wings. The desire to make my menus accessible to everyone is what inspired this chapter dedicated to meat-free dishes and sides.

Vegetarian dishes can be intimidating with their intricate directions and specialty ingredients. Don't worry—I've got your back. This chapter highlights recipes that I've collected, created or modified that can be enjoyed by most people on the vegetarian spectrum. They're also some of the favorites of the meat eaters in my immediate family! And don't fret: they are easy to prepare with easy-to-find ingredients.

If you've never prepared quinoa—a protein-laden edible seed posing as a whole grain—check out how easy it is to prepare. Turn to page 139 for the colorful, healthy and delicious Quinoa Veggie Pilaf.

Add a little Latin flair to your table with Spinach and Mozzarella Empanadas (page 156). Your kids will love eating these warm pockets oozing with flavor.

Here, you'll also find foolproof sides to round out any meal! Don't miss our family's favorites: Savory Noodle and Rice Pilaf (page 151), a nostalgic oldie-but-goodie from my mom; Creamy Corn Casserole (page 147), a comfort food featuring everyone's favorite vegetable; and Israeli Couscous with Sautéed Onions (page 143), my tour-de-force recipe that pleases both the veggie eager and the veggie hesitant.

QUINOA VEGGIE PILAF

(DF, EG, GF, NF, SF, V)

Quinoa is the darling of the health-food community: high in protein, gluten free and packed with all nine essential amino acids. Quinoa also boasts a high fiber content, which keeps you feeling fuller longer. In this recipe, sautéed veggies offset the nutty crunch of this wonder food. I like to provide some slivered or sliced almonds on the side for anyone wanting to add more protein (1 cup [170 g] of quinoa has 8 grams of protein, and 1 ounce [28 g] of almonds adds another 6 grams of protein).

No matter how you pronounce *quinoa* (I personally use the traditional *Merriam-Webster* pronunciation of 'kēn-wä), you'll be sure to call this dish de-*lish*.

Prep Time: 5 minutes   Cook Time: 15 minutes   Serves 6

In a medium saucepan, heat the olive oil over medium heat. Add the mirepoix, and sauté the vegetables for about 5 minutes.

Add the vegetable broth, quinoa and allspice to the saucepan, and stir well.

Cover the pot, reduce the heat to medium-low and cook covered for 15 minutes, or until all the liquid is absorbed into the quinoa.

Remove the pot from the heat, and let it rest for 5 minutes.

Fluff the quinoa with a fork, and stir in the chopped parsley, if using.

Season with salt as needed.

2 tablespoons (30 ml) extra-virgin olive oil

1 (12- to 16-ounce [192- to 256-g]) container mirepoix chopped vegetable mix (see Tips)

3½ cups (840 ml) vegetable broth

2 cups (340 g) quinoa

1 teaspoon ground allspice

2 tablespoons (7 g) chopped fresh parsley, optional

TIPS: I purchase the mirepoix chopped vegetable mix at my local Trader Joe's, but most grocery stores carry this. It is a mix of fresh chopped carrots, onions and celery. If you cannot find this mix, you can use 1 cup (128 g) of chopped carrots, ½ cup (80 g) of chopped yellow onion and ½ cup (51 g) of chopped celery.

If you are on a low-salt diet, you can use low-sodium vegetable or chicken broth in this recipe.

CRISPY SMASHED POTATOES WITH HONEY-MUSTARD DIP

(DF, EF, GF, NF, SF, V)

When my teenage son declared, "Mom—these are literally the best things I have ever eaten," I knew this recipe was a winner. Yes, he devoured most of the pan (one adolescent boy versus a four-serving recipe)—but the fact that he paused midway to send his Momma Chef some love? Priceless!

Make this recipe as an after-school treat as well as a fanciful side dish. While the sweet and tangy honey-mustard dip teams perfectly with these hot and crispy potatoes, you can boost the fun by serving a selection of sauces. Add up to 1 tablespoon (15 ml) of sriracha to ¼ cup (60 ml) of mayonnaise for a creamy sauce with a kick.

Prep Time: 5 minutes   Cook Time: 20 minutes   Serves 4

Preheat the oven to 425°F (218°C). Line a baking sheet with aluminum foil.

Prick each potato once using a fork, and place the potatoes on a large microwave-safe plate or platter. Microwave the potatoes on high for 5 minutes.

Place the cooked potatoes on the prepared baking sheet, and gently press each one down with the bottom of a water glass to smash. (It's OK if the potatoes come apart a little when you are smashing them. Just push them back together.)

Drizzle the olive oil over the potatoes, sprinkle with salt and pepper, and bake uncovered for 20 minutes.

While the potatoes are baking, in a small bowl, mix the mustard and honey together to make the dipping sauce.

Gently move the potatoes with a spatula to a serving dish, and serve them warm with the honey-mustard sauce on the side.

1½ pounds (450 g) small red or yellow potatoes

2 tablespoons (30 ml) extra-virgin olive oil

1 teaspoon kosher salt (see Tip)

Dash of black pepper

2 tablespoons (30 ml) Dijon mustard

2 tablespoons (30 ml) honey

TIP: In place of kosher salt, you can use truffle salt; it adds a distinct flavor to the potatoes.

ISRAELI COUSCOUS WITH SAUTÉED ONIONS

(DF, EF, NF, SF, V)

We are a divided household when it comes to rice and couscous dishes. To add veggies or to not add veggies? That is the question. For my husband and oldest son, the answer is a resounding yes. My younger two, however, like them plain. I created this recipe as a good middle ground, and I love to look around the table to see everyone enjoying it. (True, I have to close my eyes when one son picks out the onions, but then, it's all good!) Couscous—a teeny-tiny pasta—acts as a perfect base for all sorts of add-ins. If you aren't certain if you or your kids will like couscous, start with this recipe. You'll be fans after one bite! After cooking, you could add a little crunch by stirring in some toasted pine nuts, or add a little sweetness with a handful of golden raisins.

Prep Time: 5 minutes   Cook Time: 10 minutes   Serves 6

In a medium pot, heat the oil over medium-high heat. Add the onion, and sauté for 5 minutes. Add the broth and couscous. Increase the heat to high, and bring to a boil uncovered.

Once boiling, reduce the heat to low, cover and cook for 8 to 10 minutes, stirring occasionally.

Remove the pot from the heat, and fluff the couscous with a fork.

Place the couscous in a serving dish, add salt to taste, and sprinkle with parsley, if using.

1 tablespoon (15 ml) extra-virgin olive oil

1 large yellow onion, sliced very thin (see Tips)

2¼ cups (300 ml) vegetable or chicken broth

2 cups (318 g) pearl or Israeli couscous (the larger-style couscous)

2 tablespoons (7 g) finely chopped fresh Italian parsley, optional

TIPS: You can swap out the onion for 1 cup (145 g) of finely sliced shiitake mushrooms.

If there are no nut allergies, I like to lightly toast 2 tablespoons (16 g) of pine nuts and mix them into the couscous after it has finished cooking.

BARBECUE MUSHROOM "BACON"

(DF, EF, GF, NF, SF, V)

Mmmmm. Bacon.

Here, vegetarians as well as health-conscious meat eaters can enjoy the smoky flavor of bacon while avoiding the fat and other drawbacks of processed meats. The easy homemade barbecue sauce is a perfect vehicle for a few drops of liquid smoke. If you're not familiar with liquid smoke, it's a secret weapon for reproducing the flavor of cooking over a fire without spending hours tending to a barbecue pit. Now you can be the hero of vegans and meat eaters alike when you add this tasty topping to your favorite dishes. Try it on pizzas or in omelets. We love it on veggie burgers! You can also enjoy it straight up as a sensational side dish.

Prep Time: 5 minutes   Cook Time: 15 minutes   Serves 4

In a large frying pan, heat the oil over medium-high heat. Add the mushrooms, and sauté for 5 minutes.

In a small mixing bowl, add the tomato paste, brown sugar, vinegar and liquid smoke, and whisk until combined.

Pour the marinade over the mushrooms, and reduce the heat to medium.

Cook the mushrooms uncovered for 10 minutes more until the sauce has thickened and coated the mushrooms, stirring often. Serve the mushrooms hot.

1 tablespoon (15 ml) vegetable oil

1 pound (172 g) oyster or cremini (144 g) mushrooms, thinly sliced

⅓ cup (88 g) tomato paste

¼ cup (55 g) light brown sugar

¼ cup (60 ml) apple cider vinegar

1 teaspoon liquid smoke

TIP: The mushrooms will keep in an airtight container in the refrigerator for up to 3 days.

CREAMY CORN CASSEROLE

(EF, NF, SF, V)

Creamy corn casserole is a traditional Midwestern staple. Because corn is the only vegetable universally loved among my children, it's also a Momma Chef staple. (Obviously, I don't recommend this decadent casserole as the only way to serve veggies to your kiddos!) Everyone will want a spoonful or two (or three) of this favorite casserole. The corn muffin mix makes this dish truly addictive; it caramelizes as it bakes, adding a slightly sweet and mild crunch to the creamy goodness. I simply love the flexibility of this recipe, too! You can serve it in the summer with whatever you're grilling, bring it to a Thanksgiving gathering and make it for simple weeknight dinners. Some people like to splurge by adding their favorite shredded cheese before baking. I also like to have a bottle of hot sauce on hand for those eaters who prefer a little spice.

Prep Time: 5 minutes   Cook Time: 45 minutes   Serves 8

Preheat the oven to 350°F (177°C).

In a large mixing bowl, combine the whole kernel corn, cream-style sweet corn and its liquid, sour cream, eggs, corn muffin mix and melted butter.

Coat a 9 x 13–inch (23 x 33–cm) baking dish with cooking spray, and pour the corn mixture into the dish.

Bake uncovered for 45 minutes, or until the top is golden brown and set.

1 (15.25-ounce [432-g]) can sweet whole kernel corn, drained

1 (14.75-ounce [418-g]) can cream-style sweet corn

½ cup (120 ml) sour cream

2 eggs

1 cup (8 ounces [227 g]) corn muffin or cornbread mix, regular or gluten free

2 tablespoons (28 g) unsalted butter, melted

TIPS: You can use a 12-ounce (340-g) bag of frozen super sweet corn in place of the canned sweet whole kernel corn.

If you want to add cheese to this casserole, you can sprinkle 1 cup (112 g) of grated Cheddar cheese on the top before baking.

WINTER SQUASH SOUFFLÉ

(DF, NF, SF, V)

When I originally saw this dish on a dinner buffet, I mistakenly assumed that there was no more room on the dessert table. My friend corrected me, letting me know that the "pie" was actually her winter squash soufflé. I should take a piece, she said. I would like it, she said. A side of butternut squash pie? That would be a hard pass, I thought. Luckily, she persisted, finally persuading me to try a taste. And boy, am I glad I did! Slightly sweet, this soufflé pairs nicely with any main dish that I've thrown its way. Throughout the years, I've tweaked the recipe to make it easier and healthier (decreasing the sugar and substituting whole wheat flour), but it's still just as delectable. Listen to my friend: you "butter-nut" miss giving this dish a try!

Prep Time: 5 minutes   Cook Time: 45 minutes   Serves 8

Preheat the oven to 375°F (191°C).

In a large bowl, using a hand mixer on medium speed, blend together the squash, flour, sugar, eggs and margarine until well blended.

Pour the mixture into the pie crust.

Bake uncovered for 45 to 50 minutes until the top is firm and brown.

1 (10- to 12-ounce [284- to 380-g]) package frozen winter squash, defrosted and drained well

½ cup (60 g) whole wheat flour

⅓ cup (66 g) granulated sugar

3 eggs

¼ cup (60 ml) softened margarine or melted coconut oil

1 (9-inch [23-cm]) graham cracker pie crust (regular or gluten free)

TIP: You can find the package of winter squash in the freezer section of most grocery stores. If you cannot find this, you can use 1½ cups (308 g) of canned butternut squash. The squash soufflé will be a bit denser, and you need to increase the cooking time to 1 hour. I have used this before and it's a great substitution.

SAVORY NOODLE AND RICE PILAF

(EF, DF, NF, SF, V)

If you've been paying attention as you browse this cookbook, you might have picked up on a theme: I love my mom, and I love her cooking. This chapter's throwback is the pilaf we grew up eating. To this day, we all want her to bring it to every holiday gathering. Because it's a family favorite, Mom has to double the recipe—although as her grandchildren grow older and their appetites increase, soon she'll need to triple it! Something that you'll love is that it makes a tasty accompaniment to most main dishes, but it's plain enough that even the pickiest kids will love it.

Prep Time: 5 minutes   Cook Time: 20 minutes   Serves 6

In a large saucepan, heat the oil over medium-high heat. Add the noodles, and cook for 3 minutes, stirring constantly.

Add the rice, vegetable broth and onion soup mix. Stir to combine.

Bring the mixture to a boil, then cover and reduce the heat to low. Simmer for 15 to 20 minutes, or until the rice and noodles have absorbed all the liquid.

Fluff the mixture with a fork, and serve.

3 tablespoons (45 ml) extra-virgin olive oil

1 cup (56 g) fine egg noodles

2 cups (400 g) instant rice

3 cups (720 ml) vegetable broth

1 (1-ounce [27-g]) envelope onion soup mix (my favorite is Lipton Onion Soup Mix)

EGGPLANT AND SPINACH LASAGNA

(EF, GF, LC, NF, SF, V)

Creating recipes for lasagna is my happy place. I love combining layers of flavors and textures to produce perfect bites of warm, cheesy goodness. My kitchen turns into a mad scientist's lab as I experiment to find six perfect ingredients. Adding tangy artichokes to this dish was my eureka moment. You'll love how their flavor and texture make your taste buds dance for joy. The good news doesn't stop with the taste—you won't believe how *quickly* you can make this elegant lasagna! There's no boiling noodles—you just slice up some eggplant. How fabulous is that?

Prep Time: 5 minutes   Cook Time: 55 minutes   Serves 6

Preheat the oven to 375°F (191°C).

In a medium bowl, mix the spinach, ricotta and artichoke hearts.

Slice off the ends of the eggplant, and then cut it into six to eight strips lengthwise.

Pour 1 cup (240 ml) of the marinara sauce on the bottom of an 8 x 8-inch (20 x 20-cm) baking dish, and arrange half of the eggplant over the sauce. Cover the eggplant with another 1 cup (240 ml) of the sauce and half of the ricotta mixture. Repeat with the remaining eggplant, ricotta mixture and sauce.

Cover the dish with aluminum foil, and bake for 40 minutes.

Remove the dish from the oven, uncover and add the mozzarella cheese on top. Bake uncovered for 15 minutes more. Remove from the oven, and serve immediately.

1 cup (124 g) fresh spinach

1 cup (248 g) low-fat ricotta cheese

½ cup (116 g) drained, quartered or mini artichoke hearts

1 large eggplant

3 cups (720 ml) tomato-basil marinara or pasta sauce

1½ cups (168 g) shredded mozzarella

> **TIP:** If you want to add meat to this recipe, you can mix in 1 pound (454 g) of ground beef or ground turkey to the ricotta mixture.

TURMERIC-ROASTED CAULIFLOWER

(DF, EF, GF, LC, NF, SF, V)

Paleo perfection? Absolutely! Simple beauty? Check. My go-to side dish? Yes, yes, yes!

If you've never been a cauliflower fan, then you have not tried this recipe. Roasting this underappreciated vegetable transforms it from "meh" to marvelous. Adding turmeric elevates this dish to the next level. Its vibrant color changes the typically pale presentation of cauliflower into gorgeous golden-hued eye candy. Turmeric is more than just good looks, though. You won't want to miss out on the antioxidant and anti-inflammatory properties of this wonder spice. Call me shallow, though, because I totally forget all the wholesome perks of turmeric when I see how gosh-darn pretty this prepared recipe looks on my table.

Prep Time: 5 minutes   Cook Time: 20 minutes   Serves 6

Preheat the oven to 400°F (204°C). Line a baking sheet with aluminum foil. (You can also use a large disposable pan.)

In a gallon-sized zip-top bag, combine the olive oil, lemon juice, salt, turmeric and sugar.

Seal the bag and shake all the ingredients to mix.

Add the cauliflower florets, seal the bag again and shake again to coat the cauliflower.

Spread the cauliflower on the prepared baking sheet or disposable pan.

Roast for 20 minutes until the cauliflower is soft.

¼ cup (60 ml) extra-virgin olive oil

2 tablespoons (30 ml) lemon juice

1 teaspoon kosher salt (see Tips)

¼ teaspoon ground turmeric

1 tablespoon (15 g) granulated sugar

2-pound (907-g) bag cauliflower florets

TIPS: I like to sprinkle chopped fresh flat-leaf parsley over the roasted cauliflower right before serving.

You can find bagged cauliflower florets at almost all grocery stores.

If you want to bring this dish to another level, use truffle salt in place of regular salt.

SPINACH AND MOZZARELLA EMPANADAS

(NF, SF, V)

When my friend travels to New York City, she makes it a priority to hit a local diner in the Hell's Kitchen neighborhood: Empanada Mama's. At this tiny restaurant, you sit elbow-to-elbow at small chartreuse tables while Latin music fills the air and waiters serve delicious stuffed pastries. She was thrilled when I taught her that she can easily and quickly make these warm pockets of goodness in her own home! While this spinach and mozzarella combination is a classic, I know that you and your family will enjoy coming up with your own favorite combinations of ingredients for these "humble hand pies" (my favorite empanada description ever).

Prep Time: 5 minutes   Cook Time: 20 minutes   Makes 24 empanadas

Preheat the oven to 375º F. Line a baking sheet with parchment paper.

In a medium skillet, heat the oil over medium heat. Add the onion, and sauté until soft, about 2 minutes. Add the spinach and salt, mix and cook for another 3 minutes.

Remove the skillet from the heat, and let the mixture cool for about 10 minutes.

Lightly brush edges of an empanada disk with water. Place 1 tablespoon (15 ml) of the spinach mixture in the center of a disk, and top it with 1 tablespoon (2 g) of the shredded mozzarella.

Fold the wrapper over the filling, and press the edges with a fork to seal. Repeat with the remaining disks.

Arrange the empanadas on the baking sheet, and spray the tops of the empanadas with cooking spray.

Bake uncovered for 20 minutes until crisp and lightly brown.

1 tablespoon (15 ml) extra-virgin olive oil

½ cup (80 g) finely diced onion

1 (10-ounce [283-g]) package frozen spinach, thawed and well drained

½ teaspoon kosher salt

20 empanada disks (see Tips)

2 cups (224 g) shredded mozzarella

> **TIPS:** You can usually find the empanada disks or dough in the freezer section of your grocery store.
>
> In place of empanada dough, you can use puff pastry or wonton wrappers.

VEGETARIAN BLACK BEAN CHILI

(DF, EF, GF, NF, SF, V)

Chicago can be bone-chilling cold. The kind of cold that makes even the most virtuous person swear like a sailor when being lambasted by the icy winds of Lake Michigan. Whenever the temps dip below your personal threshold, I suggest that you put on a pair of thick, cozy socks and make a ginormous pot of this chili. How ginormous, you ask? It's easy to double or triple this recipe. In fact, we've been known to make enough to serve more than 100 people at *Momma Chef*'s Soup Kitchen. Refried beans give this recipe its signature "tastes like it's been simmering all day" consistency. Each of the six ingredients has a long shelf life, so be sure to stock your pantry. You'll be equipped to make a batch whenever you're craving something warm and hearty.

Prep Time: 5 minutes   Cook Time: 45 minutes   Serves 8

In a soup pot over medium heat, add the tomatoes, chili seasoning and refried beans. Stir until everything is mixed well, about 2 minutes.

Add the black beans, kidney beans and onion soup mix to the pot. Mix everything together, and bring to a boil uncovered.

Once boiling, reduce the heat to low, cover the pot and simmer the chili for 45 minutes, stirring occasionally.

Serve the chili hot.

1 (28-ounce [794-g]) can crushed tomatoes

1 (1.25-ounce [35-g]) packet mild chili seasoning

1 (16-ounce [453-g]) can vegetarian refried beans

2 (15.5-ounce [439-g]) cans seasoned black beans, drained

1 (15.5-ounce [439-g]) can dark red kidney beans, drained

1 (1-ounce [27-g]) envelope onion soup mix (my favorite is Lipton Onion Soup Mix)

> **TIPS:** You can add any topping to your bowl of chili. Our favorites are shredded Cheddar cheese and freshly chopped onions.
>
> This chili is mild. If you want to add some heat, you can add ½ teaspoon of red pepper flakes (more or less, to taste) when you add the chili seasoning.

WHAT'S IN YOUR KITCHEN?

Once upon a time, my family and I unexpectedly found ourselves sheltering in place for a seemingly infinite number of days.

After the first week or so, the novelty wore off and some stress set in. Everyone everywhere was trying to navigate our "new normal." For me, that meant searching for solace and direction in my happy place: the kitchen. When I think back to those initial days, I remember a lot of somewhat aimless circulating: taking stock of what was in the refrigerator, pantry, freezer and cupboards. Like a robot on autopilot, I did daily checks of expiration dates, purged, reorganized and made lists for our weekly grocery curbside pickup order. As this daily routine turned into daily monotony, I searched for a way to challenge myself to hold the anxiety at bay. My solution was to invent the cleverly named game—*pause for imaginary studio audience to shout it out*—*"Karen! What's In Your Kitchen?"*

The goal? To create recipes using only the ingredients found in my home. Going to the store to make a purchase for the recipe would result in a disqualification. This "game" invigorated and humbled me. I realized how often I had relied on being able to jump in the car to pick up a missing ingredient or two for a meal. I was reminded of the discipline of making the best use of what I already had on my shelves. This chapter highlights some of the winning recipes.

I'm especially proud of the desserts here. My 20-year-old self would applaud my current self for Nutella Cheesecake Bars (page 176). I went to college before the days of Grubhub or Uber Eats. Back then, if you had a late-night craving for something sweet, you were on your own: You had to make do with what was in your efficiency kitchen in your college apartment. Oh, how I wish I could time-travel back with a tray of these to push us through the occasional all-nighter.

Fast forward to the future, and you'll find the No-Bake Fruit Tart (page 179) is a delightful dessert to bring to any occasion. But there's no need to wait for a special event to make it. It's a perfect choice for those times when you have that fruit in your produce drawer that is not quite languishing, but will be soon. Half-empty containers of strawberries and blueberries? Sounds like it's time to make a tart!

Craving some comfort carbs? With just a few ingredients already in your kitchen, you can indulge in a Creamy Enchilada Skillet Pasta (page 163) for a warm and filling meal.

I hope this chapter's remaining simple dinners, sides, soups, appetizer and Silky Chocolate Pie (page 180) will inspire you to play your own rounds of "What's In Your Kitchen?" Enjoy the process, and maybe you'll create a new dinner favorite. Get inspired to see how creative and resilient we can be when we find ourselves stuck at home—for a day, a week or a season of our lives.

CREAMY ENCHILADA SKILLET PASTA

(NF, SF, V)

"I have so much time to cook dinner for my busy family," said no one ever. Whenever possible, I work to streamline my recipes to save families time. Case in point: the pasta in this recipe is boiled directly in the sauce. That's one fewer pan to clean! In fact, this recipe turned out to be a dream come true for my friend's family. Last month, her daughter was hankering for some enchiladas, but they were struggling to find time in their busy schedules to prepare the labor-intensive dish. When she shared her dilemma with me, I gave her a sneak peek of this recipe to take on a test drive. Their review: *Enchilada sauce with pasta? Genius! It was exactly the taste we were craving. Five stars from our test kitchen to yours!*

Prep Time: 5 minutes   Cook Time: 20 minutes   Serves 6

In a large skillet over medium heat, combine the enchilada sauce and vegetable broth, and bring to a boil.

Once boiling, reduce the heat to medium-low, and mix in the taco seasoning. Add the pasta and corn, and stir.

Cover and simmer for 20 to 25 minutes until the pasta is tender, stirring occasionally and making sure the pasta is not sticking to the bottom of the skillet.

Once the pasta is tender, remove from the heat, and add in the shredded cheese. Mix everything together, and serve immediately.

2 cups (280 ml) red enchilada sauce

1 (32-ounce [960-ml]) box vegetable broth

1 tablespoon (14 g) mild taco seasoning

1 (16-ounce [453-g]) box orecchiette pasta (see Tips)

1 cup (226 g) frozen white or yellow kernel corn (see Tips)

1½ cups (170 g) shredded Mexican-style cheese

TIPS: If you can't find orecchiette pasta, you can use shell pasta. Do not use whole wheat pasta in this recipe; it will come out sticky.

You can also add ground beef to this recipe. Add 1 pound (454 g) of ground beef, and mix it in when you add in the cheese.

You can swap out the corn for other yummy additions, such as black beans or fresh spinach.

GRILLED ESPRESSO-GLAZED CHICKEN

(DF, EF, GF, NF, SF)

Words cannot espresso how much you're going to love this crave-worthy dish!

In 2020, social media ignited a whipped coffee fad, leaving many of us with half-empty jars of instant coffee crystals. Every fad has a silver lining, though. Those coffee crystals inspired one of our favorite summer meals: espresso-glazed chicken. Don't worry—the marinade doesn't taste like a cup of joe. The instant coffee gives the chicken a dark, delicious flavor, but the coffee flavor burns off when cooking. If you have an espresso maker, you can replace the crystals with a shot, and you will still love it a *latte*.

I love making this dish with boneless, skinless chicken thighs; they stay extra tender on the grill.

Prep Time: 3 minutes   Cook Time: 12 minutes   Serves 6

In a gallon-sized zip-top bag, combine the honey, teriyaki sauce, garlic, paprika and instant coffee.

Seal the bag and lightly shake it to combine the ingredients.

Add the chicken thighs to the bag, seal the bag and shake again, making sure the chicken is coated in the marinade.

Put the bag in the refrigerator, and let the chicken marinate for at least 2 hours or up to overnight.

When you're ready to cook, preheat the grill to medium. Remove the chicken from the marinade, and grill the chicken until it is cooked through, approximately 6 minutes on each side or until a meat thermometer reads 165°F (74°C).

¼ cup (60 ml) honey

½ cup (120 ml) teriyaki sauce (regular or gluten free)

3 cloves garlic, minced

2 teaspoons (5 g) ground sweet paprika

1 teaspoon instant coffee dissolved in ¼ cup (60 ml) hot water

2 pounds (907 g) boneless, skinless chicken thighs or breasts

TIP: You can use boneless, skinless chicken breasts instead of chicken thighs. They tend to be larger, so you will need to grill the chicken a couple more minutes on each side.

MEDITERRANEAN GREEN BEANS IN TOMATO SAUCE

(DF, EF, GF, NF, SF, V)

The Mediterranean diet is the sweetheart of doctors and diners who want to eat healthy without sacrificing taste. This simple green bean dish exemplifies one of the tasty and heart-healthy dishes that include the dynamic duo of Mediterranean cuisine: a little olive oil and a lot of vegetables. The contrasting colors of the dish brighten up any table—from a festive side at a summer picnic to an elegant addition to a holiday table. *Buon appetito!*

Prep Time: 5 minutes   Cook Time: 10 minutes   Serves 6

In a large frying pan, heat the olive oil. Add in the shallot and garlic, and cook for about 3 minutes.

Add the green beans, crushed tomatoes with their juices and salt to the pan, and mix well.

Cover the pan, and cook for 10 minutes, stirring occasionally until the green beans are soft.

Remove from the heat, season with salt as needed, and serve immediately.

2 tablespoons (30 ml) extra-virgin olive oil

1 shallot, sliced

3 cloves garlic, sliced

1 pound (454 g) fresh green beans, ends trimmed

1 (15-ounce [425-g]) can crushed tomatoes

1 teaspoon kosher salt, plus more to taste

> **TIPS:** For a bit of spice, you can add in ½ teaspoon of red pepper flakes when cooking.
>
> One of my boys likes to squeeze lemon juice on the green beans when they are done cooking. If you have any hesitant eaters, let them try this—It worked for me!

BAKED MOZZARELLA STICKS

(GF, NF, SF, V)

It's cold here in Chicagoland. In mid-January, the temps are plummeting, the wind is howling, and the snow is blowing—only the brave want to venture outside. For my family, the onset of winter weather ups our craving for comfort food. The juicy and refreshing fruit that we relished in June has been replaced by our need for ooey, gooey deliciousness. Cue the mozzarella sticks. My boys' eyes light up when they come in from the cold and find a tray waiting for them, hot out of the oven. And now that my boys are older, the recipe is easy enough that they can make a second tray on their own! It's the perfect snack—filled with protein, calcium and cheesy goodness. If you wish, you can use low-fat mozzarella to cut the calories.

Prep Time: 5 minutes   Cook Time: 7 minutes   Makes 16 mozzarella sticks

Cut each stick of string cheese in half to give you 16 pieces, and place them in the freezer until the cheese is frozen, at least 1 hour.

When you're ready to bake, preheat the oven to 400°F (204°C). Line a baking sheet with aluminum foil and lightly coat the foil with cooking spray.

In a large bowl, mix the egg and milk. Set aside.

In a gallon-sized zip-top bag, add the breadcrumbs and salt.

Dip each frozen string cheese in the egg mixture, and put them in the zip-top bag.

Seal the bag and shake to coat all sides of the cheese.

Arrange the breaded cheese sticks in a single layer on the prepared baking sheet, and bake uncovered for 7 minutes.

8 sticks mozzarella string cheese

1 egg, beaten

1 tablespoon (15 ml) milk

½ cup (28 g) seasoned breadcrumbs (you can also use gluten-free panko)

¼ teaspoon kosher salt

TIP: My kids like dipping these in marinara sauce or ranch dressing.

SUMMER BROCCOLI AND RAISIN SALAD

(DF, GF, NF, SF, V)

Ummm . . . so . . . the serving size for this recipe is eight, but let's be real. Fans of broccoli salads will eat this by the bowlful, so plan accordingly. It's best if you can stave off the temptation of this tangy and crunchy concoction by giving the flavors a chance to meld by letting it chill for at least 30 minutes. Epitomizing the spirit of the "What's In Your Kitchen?" chapter, this recipe begs you to personalize it by experimenting with what's in your pantry and refrigerator. Play around with the add-ins! We've used dried cranberries, sunflower seeds, pumpkin seeds, walnuts, "fried onion" topping and shredded carrots. You can also ramp it up with your leftover protein from the night before—some shredded chicken or cubed meat will transform this salad from a tasty side dish to a satisfying lunch. Stir in any crunchy toppings just before serving.

Prep Time: 5 minutes   Serves 8

In a large salad bowl, combine the broccoli, raisins and onion.

In a small mixing bowl, add the mayonnaise, sugar and vinegar, and mix until well combined.

Pour the mayonnaise mixture over the broccoli mixture, and toss everything together.

Serve this immediately, or let it sit in the refrigerator for 30 minutes to let the flavors combine.

12-ounce (137-g) bag fresh broccoli florets

1 cup (160 g) raisins

1 small red onion, chopped

¾ cup (180 ml) mayonnaise (regular or low fat)

¼ cup (50 g) granulated sugar

2 tablespoons (30 ml) apple cider vinegar

WINTER VEGETABLE AND LENTIL STEW

(DF, EF, GF, NF, SF, V)

Do you have a rogue bag of lentils, forgotten in the back of your cupboard? Or maybe you've always wanted to buy them, but you've been looking for the right recipe. The time has come to grab your lentils and make this delicious and nourishing stew. People have been cooking with these magic legumes for thousands of years, and it's time you got on board using this tasty recipe. FYI: I debated long and hard about jazzing up this recipe's name to something more tantalizing. The top nomination was *"My-Husband-Says-This-Is-Amazing Vegetable and Lentil Stew."* He might be my biggest fan but I'm telling you, if my dear hubby loves it, you're going to love it, too.

Prep Time: 5 minutes   Cook Time: 45 minutes   Serves 6

In a large soup pot, heat the olive oil over medium-high heat. Sauté the onion for 3 minutes.

Add the lentils and frozen vegetables, and sauté for 2 minutes more.

Add the vegetable broth and the can of tomatoes with their juices, and bring to a boil.

Reduce the heat to low, partially cover the pot and cook until the lentils are soft, about 45 minutes.

2 tablespoons (30 ml) extra-virgin olive oil

1 medium yellow onion, chopped

1 cup (192 g) dry brown or green lentils, rinsed

1 (12-ounce [340-g]) bag frozen vegetables (Italian or Mediterranean blend)

1 (48-ounce [1.4-L]) box vegetable broth

1 (14.5-ounce [411-g]) can diced tomatoes

CREAMY TOMATO SOUP

The smell of this soup stirs up some of the happiest of my 1980-something child-hood memories. In Kodachrome color, I can see myself on our backyard playset. I determinedly pump my legs, the swing going higher and higher. I reach that perfect spot where the metal leg of the playset starts to lift a bit out of the ground. In my Care Bear shirt and my Smurfs shoes, the wind blowing my hair, I feel reckless, dangerous, invincible. My mom calls me in for lunch, and I fly off the swing and run inside where a cup of tomato soup, a grilled cheese sandwich and an episode of *Fraggle Rock* await. Ah, nostalgic bliss. I hope my kids are building beautiful olfactory memories of their own with each whiff of the comforting aroma of this creamy soup. Give this recipe a try, and you'll never go back to canned soup again.

Prep Time: 5 minutes   Cook Time: 25 minutes   Serves 6

In a large soup pot, heat the olive oil over medium heat. Add the onion, and sauté for 3 minutes.

Add the tomatoes, vegetable broth and basil.

Simmer uncovered for 25 minutes.

Puree the soup in batches in a blender, food processor or using an immersion blender until smooth.

Stir in the cream, and serve immediately, or store in the refrigerator for up to 3 days until ready to serve.

2 tablespoons (30 ml) extra-virgin olive oil

1 yellow onion, chopped

1 (28-ounce [794-g]) can crushed tomatoes

1 (32-ounce [960-ml]) box vegetable broth

½ cup (12 g) fresh basil, stems removed

½ cup (120 ml) heavy cream or half-and-half

TIPS: This recipe can be made dairy free by omitting the cream or using almond or cashew milk (making sure there are no tree-nut allergies).

Make sure you blend this soup so the kiddos don't see the basil or pieces of tomato.

NUTELLA CHEESECAKE BARS

(GF, NF, SF, V)

This easy dessert is a great way to celebrate World Nutella Day on February 5. It's also a great way to celebrate Mondays. Or Thursdays. Or partly cloudy days. Or even-numbered days. You get the picture. Should you tire (*gasp*) of Nutella, you can easily substitute with your favorite fruit jam. Might I suggest raspberry jam as the perfect berry partner of cheesecake? And since you asked—the answer is yes—of course, you can indulge by eating a slice for a breakfast treat. Whether Nutella based or fruit infused, these bars go great with a cup of coffee.

Prep Time: 5 minutes   Cook Time: 55 minutes   Serves 6

Preheat the oven to 350°F (177°C).

Spoon the Nutella into the pie crust, making sure the Nutella covers the entire bottom of the crust.

In a large mixing bowl, beat the eggs with a hand mixer on medium speed for 30 seconds.

Add the cream cheese, sugar and vanilla to the eggs, and blend on medium speed until smooth, about 3 minutes.

Pour the cream cheese mixture into the pie crust on top of the Nutella, and bake uncovered for 55 minutes until the center is firm.

Let the cheesecake cool in the refrigerator for at least 1 hour, and then cut it into triangles or bars.

⅓ cup (86 g) Nutella

1 (9-inch [23-cm]) graham cracker pie crust (regular or gluten free)

2 eggs

2 (8-ounce [232-g]) packages cream cheese, at room temperature (see Tips)

½ cup (100 g) granulated sugar

2 teaspoons (10 ml) vanilla extract

TIPS: You can use regular or low-fat cream cheese in this recipe; do not use the fat-free version.

If you like Nutella, you should also check out my recipe for Nutella Crepes on page 70.

NO-BAKE FRUIT TART

(EF, GF, NF, SF, V)

You'll want to turn to this recipe again and again for two big reasons. The first? Easy! It's downright delicious. The second? It's the best arts-and-crafts project ever. Go simple or go glam! Fruit is your medium, and Cool Whip is your canvas. When you decorate the tart, you can be as creative or random as you wish. Channel your inner Frida Kahlo and create a masterpiece of symmetry and beauty. Running late? Toss some berries on the whipped cream à la Jackson Pollock. Use blueberries and strawberries to create a charming patriotic dessert to pass around a Fourth of July potluck. Pair strawberries and raspberries to fashion an elegant design for an engagement, shower or anniversary.

Prep Time: 5 minutes   Serves 6

In a medium bowl, add the graham crackers and butter, and mix well.

Press the graham cracker mixture firmly into a pie pan, and refrigerate for 30 minutes.

Remove the pie pan from the refrigerator, and spread the strawberry jam on the crust.

Add the Cool Whip on top of the jam.

Lay the berries on the Cool Whip in a single layer.

Eat immediately, or refrigerate to serve later in the day.

TIP: You can easily make this recipe dairy free by using margarine in place of butter and a coconut-based Cool Whip.

1½ cups (180 g) crushed graham crackers, regular or gluten free

⅓ cup (75 g) unsalted butter, melted (see Tip)

½ cup (120 ml) strawberry jam (not jelly)

1 (8-ounce [226-g]) container Cool Whip

1 cup (120 to 150 g) fresh berries of your choice

SILKY CHOCOLATE PIE

(GF, NF, SF, V)

The characters: My son and his friends

The setting: A backyard pickup football game

The conflict: Teenage appetites and a gluten-free linebacker

The resolution: Everyone's a winner with this silky chocolate pie!

Give yourself enough time to chill this pie for at least an hour before serving—by far, the most difficult challenge of this dish. My teen judges were far more indulgent than the notorious Paul Hollywood of *The Great British Bake Off*. They devoured it with goofy grins. I guarantee that this recipe will earn you the title of "star baker" from your friends and family.

Prep Time: 5 minutes   Cook Time: 5 minutes   Serves 6

In a large saucepan over medium heat, add the milk, and bring to a boil.

Once the milk is boiling, reduce the heat to medium-low, and whisk in the eggs, sugar, cocoa powder and cornstarch. Whisk until everything is well combined.

Cook until the mixture is thick, whisking constantly, for about 5 minutes.

Let the mixture cool in the saucepan for about 10 minutes, and then pour the mixture into the pie crust.

Refrigerate for at least 1 hour, or until the pie is cooled and firm.

2 cups (480 ml) whole milk

2 eggs

1 cup (200 g) granulated sugar

½ cup (50 g) cocoa powder

¼ cup (32 g) cornstarch

1 (9-inch [23-cm]) graham cracker pie crust (regular or gluten free)

TIP: Before serving this, I like to add some whipped cream on top, or you can try sliced strawberries or marshmallows. The possibilities are endless.

COOKING WITH KIDS

Kids love to create, and the kitchen is a perfect place for them to learn new skills. I designed these recipes for grown-ups and kids to work side by side. Children will have the pleasure of preparing (and eating) yummy treats, and adults will have the satisfaction of knowing they are equipping a new generation with the foundations of cooking competency. These recipes will also empower older children to work independently to prepare tasty dishes. The skill set needed for the recipes here ranges from the super easy—sprinkling toppings in Spooky Halloween Chocolate Bark (page 194)—to developing basic knife skills in Cinnamon-Apple Crisp (page 202). Of course, all these recipes can be made solo! Sometimes, it's way easier to not have a "helper."

Lifelong memories will be created when you make Homemade "Snow" Cones (page 198). I remember how fascinated I was when I read about Laura Ingalls making snow candy with her Ma in the Little House on the Prairie series. Kids will always remember the first time they make dessert with real snow!

Shout-out to my son for creating the recipe that we use the most: Tortizza! (page 186). Kids of all ages will love making crispy individual pizzas using flour tortillas as the crusts. They're such a favorite that I've made them with oodles of eager kid cooks at summer camp. This recipe is one of many that includes kids' choice of toppings, encouraging creativity and experimentation.

Of course, cooking with a helper is about more than just preparing food. You're a role model, a teacher, a cooking partner and a listener. Something I particularly value is when my sons and I are cooking together, none of us are distracted by our screens. It's a welcome treat to be fully present in the moment. The kitchen offers a safe environment that fosters both little and big conversations. Wonderful side-by-side discussions organically happen when your cooking partner (ages 6 to 96) washes fruit while you chop vegetables. You might want to pick out a few recipes to make at a time—6 minutes of prep time together won't be enough! And guess what, friends—all the recipes in this chapter can be made gluten free! Make sure to read the gluten-free ingredient options.

SB & J "SUSHI" ROLLS

(DF, EF, GF, NF, SF, V)

I am not the mom who sends her kids to school with a bento box packed full of Pinterest-worthy lunch items. Imagine my surprise when this simple recipe exalted me to rockstar status in the school cafeteria. These little sushi rolls became such a favorite that one of the teachers sought me out just to thank me for the idea. She ended up making them for her daughter's birthday party, and they were a huge hit— all the guests loved them. And what's not to love about SB & J Sushi Rolls? They're cute, they're ridiculously easy and they're super hip with the tweens and teens.

Let me also point out that they're safe for kiddos with nut allergies because you make them with sunflower seed butter instead of nut butter. Teach your kids how to roll out the bread, and soon they'll be making these all on their own.

Prep Time: 5 minutes   Serves 2

Using a knife, trim the crusts from the bread slices.

Using a rolling pin, flatten the bread slices.

Spread 1 teaspoon of the sunflower seed butter on each slice of bread within ½ inch (1.3 cm) of the edges, then spread 1 teaspoon of the jam on top of the sunflower seed butter.

Roll up each slice of bread into a tight spiral. Transfer to a plate, and refrigerate for 15 minutes.

Cut each slice into 2-inch (5-cm) pieces, and serve right away, or pack into a lunchbox.

2 slices white or whole wheat bread, regular or gluten free

2 teaspoons (10 g) creamy sunflower seed butter, such as SunButter

2 teaspoons (10 ml) jam or jelly of choice

> **TIPS:** Of course, if your family does not have nut allergies, you can use any nut butter of your choosing; my kids' preference is the good standby—creamy peanut butter.
>
> This is the perfect activity for your kids when you hear those dreaded words, "I'm *bored*," or "I'm *hungry*." Just show them once how to flatten and roll the bread and they should be able to make this recipe on their own.

TORTILLA PIZZAS "TORTIZZA!"

(EF, GF, NF, SF, V)

My house is always filled with kids—mostly hungry, growing boys who constantly crave snacks. My oldest son came up with a great idea—Tortilla Pizza or, as the boys dubbed it, "tortizza"—and it has become a quick, easy and budget-friendly pick. Everyone loves the power of choosing their own toppings. I enjoy seeing how creative and adventurous kids will be when given free rein to experiment with the ingredients in the refrigerator. We've used lunch meat, leftovers and all sorts of veggies. Just make sure the kids don't overload the tortillas to ensure an even bake. And do *not* put away the ingredients—they'll definitely be asking for another tortizza, please!

Prep Time: 3 minutes   Cook: 7 minutes   Makes 1 tortizza

Preheat the oven to 400°F (204°C).

Spread the marinara evenly over the tortilla.

Sprinkle the cheese evenly over the sauce, and add your toppings.

Place the tortilla on a small pizza pan or directly on the middle oven rack.

Bake uncovered until the cheese is melted and golden and the tortillas are crispy, about 5 to 7 minutes.

¼ cup (60 ml) marinara sauce

1 flour tortilla, regular or gluten free

¼ cup (28 g) shredded mozzarella cheese

¼ cup toppings of choice (diced peppers and olives go great on these)

NO-BOIL MAC AND CHEESE

(GF, NF, SF, V)

Hush, now, and I will let you in on a Momma Chef secret—when my kids were little, they ate *gasp* boxed mac and cheese. I mean—a LOT of boxed mac and cheese. Sure, I (mostly) bought the all-natural, organic brands to balance out my guilt from the unnecessary ingredients they were putting in their little bodies by the bowl full. I became obsessed with finding an easy way to make homemade mac and cheese, the kind of mac and cheese that almost brings you to tears because it is so rich and delish. My quest was to be able to skip the step of boiling the noodles. I wanted to streamline it from mixing bowl directly to baking dish. After searching and testing and tweaking, I finally found my holy grail of no-boil baked mac and cheese. This recipe is so unbelievably easy that it actually makes the store-bought directions look difficult. Huzzah! Our boxed mac and cheese days are over.

Your kids will love to help make it, but you'll need to be on hand to transfer the heavy dish in and out of the oven.

Prep Time: 5 minutes   Cook Time: 55 minutes   Serves 8

Preheat the oven to 350°F (177°C). Spray a 9 x 13-inch (23 x 33-cm) baking dish with cooking spray.

In a large bowl, add the macaroni, milk, salt, butter and 3 cups (336 g) of the cheese, and mix well.

Pour the mixture into the prepared baking dish.

Sprinkle the remaining 2 cups (224 g) of cheese over the mixture, and cover with foil.

Bake covered for 35 minutes, then remove the foil and bake uncovered 20 minutes more.

2 cups (227 g) elbow macaroni, regular or gluten free

4 cups (960 ml) 2 percent or whole milk

1 teaspoon kosher salt

3 tablespoons (42 g) salted butter, melted

5 cups (560 g) shredded Cheddar cheese, divided

SPINACH-APPLE SALAD WITH HEAD-OVER-HEELS HONEY DRESSING

(DF, EF, GF, NF, SF, V)

Oh, honey! You're the bee's knees! Honey provides the secret ingredient in this heavenly dressing that elevates this spinach salad to the next level. Its sweetness adds a harmonious contrast to the tart apple cider vinegar and earthy garlic. Not only will you love the dressing drizzled over this recipe, you'll also want to make extra to serve on salads all week. When kids help make this salad (or any salad for that matter), odds are that they'll give it a try. Cooks like to sample their creations! For picky eaters, this recipe provides a tempting gateway to eating spinach by adding dried apples and fresh strawberries. In fact, don't be surprised if your kids start calling this recipe "that one veggie and apple salad" instead of "spinach salad."

Younger children can be given the job of tearing the spinach leaves into bite-sized pieces to make it easier for them to enjoy this iron-rich and tasty treat. Older kids can enjoy the hands-on science experiment as they combine liquids of varying densities in the dressing preparation.

Prep Time: 5 minutes   Serves 4

Add the spinach to a large salad bowl.

Top with the sliced dried apples and strawberries.

In a small bowl, mix together the honey, garlic and vinegar.

When you're ready to serve the salad, pour the dressing over the salad, and mix until well combined.

10 ounces (155 g) fresh baby spinach, washed

1 cup (160 g) dried unsweetened apples, diced into ½-inch (1.3-cm) pieces

½ cup (72 g) fresh strawberries, quartered

¼ cup (60 ml) honey

3 cloves garlic, minced

⅓ cup (80 ml) apple cider vinegar

SCRUMPTIOUS MANDARIN ORANGE CAKE

(DF, GF, NF, SF, V)

Something that I learned in 2020 was that I definitely do not want to homeschool my kids. Ever. One silver lining was that my then 7-year-old son grew leaps and bounds as a mini-chef. At his request, we added "baking time with Mom" into his morning schedule. Now, *this* was a class I loved teaching! We made a lot of Nutella-based recipes. One day, he wondered what we could do with a can of mandarin oranges. Skipping the Nutella trend, we created this cake. For budding cooks with a short attention span, the prep only took 5 minutes: It was finished before my oven preheated!

I would definitely give my son an A+ on his baking assignment. The cake was moist and delicious, and boy did it make our house smell terrific!

Prep Time: 5 minutes   Cook Time: 35 minutes   Serves 8

Preheat the oven to 350°F (177°C).

Coat a 9 x 13–inch (23 x 33–cm) baking dish or a 10-inch (25-cm) Bundt cake pan with cooking spray.

In a large bowl, combine the cake mix, eggs, oil and vanilla, and beat until smooth, about 2 minutes. Add the mandarin oranges with their juices, and lightly fold them into the cake mixture until well blended.

Pour the batter into the prepared baking dish or cake pan.

Bake uncovered for 35 to 40 minutes, or until a toothpick inserted into the center of the cake comes out clean. Allow the cake to cool.

1 (15- to 18-ounce [425- to 510-g]) package yellow cake mix, regular or gluten free

3 eggs

½ cup (120 ml) avocado or canola oil

1 teaspoon vanilla extract

1 (11-ounce [312-g]) can mandarin oranges

TIP: This cake is super easy to make gluten free. Just be sure to purchase a box of gluten-free yellow cake mix, and follow the same instructions above.

SPOOKY HALLOWEEN CHOCOLATE BARK

(EF, GF, NF, SF, V)

This recipe should really be called "Best Last-Minute Dessert" or maybe "Insert Holiday Here" Bark. The most accurate might be "I Bet You Can Make This Right Now" Chocolate Bark, because odds are you already have on hand what you need to stir up this batch of yumminess. The only must-have ingredient is a partial bag of chocolate chips—that's it! From there, you are limited only by what's in your cupboards. No matter the season, this is one of the first desserts you can make with the littlest of kids. You—of course—will be in charge of melting and spreading the heated chocolate, and they'll be in charge of dropping in their favorite mix-ins. If you're like me—multiple kids/adults with multiple palates—you can make smaller pans of chocolate bark, and each one of your little goblins can customize their toppings.

Prep Time: 5 minutes   Serves 6

In a microwave-safe bowl, add the chocolate chips, and microwave on high for 1 minute and 30 seconds.

Mix and microwave for another 1 minute until all chocolate is melted.

Coat an 8 x 8-inch (20 x 20-cm) baking dish with cooking spray, and spread the chocolate evenly around the dish. Then drop in the candy corn and M&M's.

Refrigerate the bark for at least 30 minutes until set, and then break up the chocolate bark.

1 cup (168 g) semisweet chocolate chips

20 pieces candy corn

1 small bag of M&M's (I like to use the 1.69-ounce [48-g] bag)

> **TIP:** Some other fun variations are:
> - Rice Krispies and a pinch of sea salt
> - Salted pretzel pieces and M&M's Minis
> - Marshmallows and raisins
> - A couple of handfuls of crushed candy canes
> - The combinations are endless. . . .

CREAMY NO-CHURN OREO ICE CREAM

(EF, GF, NF, SF, V)

If you have a friend who grew up in the South, chances are they have some recollection of making homemade ice cream. Grandma would get out the old wooden churn, an uncle would pull a bag of rock salt from his truck and everyone would take a turn at the crank. Nothing tasted more like summer than the first bites of homemade peach ice cream. Life is easier today, but you can still enjoy the sweet pleasure of making your own homemade ice cream with this recipe. The taste is extra-special when it's a labor of love, rather than a no-effort scoop from a cardboard container in the freezer.

Use your judgment if your helper is strong enough—and coordinated enough—to use the hand mixer. If not, crushing Oreos is a task for any age.

Prep Time: 5 minutes   Serves 6

In a large mixing bowl, with a hand mixer on medium speed, beat the heavy cream until you have stiff peaks, about 3 minutes.

Slowly blend in the condensed milk, vanilla and Oreo cookies into the bowl with the whipped cream. Only blend this for about 1 minute on low speed so you do not overmix.

Pour the cream mixture into a 9 x 3-inch (23 x 7-cm) loaf pan, or any pan that is approximately the same size but at least 3 inches (7 cm) high.

Cover the pan with plastic wrap, and freeze for at least 4 hours or up to overnight.

2 cups (480 ml) heavy cream

1 (14-ounce [396-g]) can sweetened condensed milk

1 tablespoon (15 ml) vanilla extract

1 cup (100 g) Oreo cookies, chopped, regular or gluten free

TIP: Our favorite flavor for this ice cream is Oreo, but you can mix in any of your favorites. Other yummy ideas are chopped Reese's Peanut Butter Cups or edible cookie dough.

HOMEMADE "SNOW" CONES

(DF, EF, GF, NF, SF, V)

If you're a worrier (and aren't we all?), you might wonder about the safety of eating snow. My family has been enjoying this frozen treat for years, but just to be sure, I went on an extensive deep dive of the most up-to-date scientific research about eating snow. The verdict? Relax! It's absolutely fine to eat fresh snow cones—just be smart about what snow you eat. Remind your helpers to collect snow that's clean and white (obviously) and located as far away from a road or snow-plowed route as possible. It's best to make this recipe immediately after (or during) a fresh fall. While the syrup cools, bundle up your helpers and head outside. Review the guidelines, give them plastic cups and off they go! At this point, your job is purely quality control. If their cups of snow pass inspection, add them to your bowl. Your goal is 10 cups (2.3 L) of frozen treasure. Head inside to finish the recipe stat before your snow melts!

Prep Time: 5 minutes   Cook Time: 5 minutes   Makes 5 snow cones

In a saucepan, mix the water and sugar, and bring to a boil. Stir occasionally for about 2 minutes until the sugar is dissolved. Remove from the heat.

Divide the syrup into two bowls. In one bowl, squirt about 8 drops of Kool-Aid Liquid Cherry.

In the other bowl, do the same with the Kool-Aid Liquid Grape until you've reached your desired color.

Put the bowls in the refrigerator, and chill until the liquid is cold. When it's ready, take your kids outside and have them scoop about 10 cups (2.3 L) of fresh snow into a large container (this will make about 5 snow cones). *Make sure it's clean snow!*

Put the snow into a 1-cup (240-ml) measuring cup, and press down until the snow is compact.

Keep filling until the cup is full. Turn the cup over, shape it into a ball and put the snowball into a bowl or snow cone cup. Spoon the Kool-Aid flavors over the snow.

1 cup (240 ml) water

1 cup (200 g) granulated sugar

2 (1.62-oz [49-ml]) bottles Kool-Aid Liquid Drink Mix (I like cherry and grape)

10 cups (2.3 L) clean snow

TIP: The syrup is good for 10 or more snow cones. When finished, store any leftover syrup in an airtight container in the refrigerator for up to 1 month.

PERFECT PINEAPPLE CAKE

(DF, NF, SF, V)

Life can be busy, busy, busy. A thousand blessings on the heads of the mythical Betty Crocker and the actual Duncan Hines for mass-producing cake mixes to make our lives easier. However, if your helpers have only baked from boxes, this recipe is about to blow their little minds. As for my mind, I have 95 percent convinced myself that this cake is sorta, kinda healthy. In any case, it's healthier than it could be—especially if you choose avocado oil with its heart-healthy fat and carotenoids. Sure, the crushed pineapple is in heavy syrup, but that's still a far better choice than a trans-fat can of frosting. In any case, you're about to make—and eat—a moist and delicious cake.

Prep Time: 5 minutes   Cook Time: 45 minutes   Serves 8

Preheat the oven to 350°F (177°C). Coat a 9 x 13–inch (23 x 33–cm) pan or a 10-inch (25-cm) Bundt cake pan with cooking spray.

In a large bowl, combine the flour, baking soda and brown sugar. Then add the eggs and oil. Using a hand mixer on medium speed, beat until smooth, about 2 minutes.

Pour in the can of pineapple with its juices, and with a spoon, gently mix until everything is well combined.

Pour the batter into the prepared pan. Bake uncovered for 45 minutes, or until a toothpick inserted into the center of the cake comes out clean. Allow the cake to cool.

2½ cups (313 g) all-purpose or 1:1 gluten-free flour

1 teaspoon baking soda

1½ cups (330 g) light brown sugar

2 eggs

⅓ cup (80 ml) avocado or canola oil

1 (20-ounce [567-g]) can crushed pineapple in heavy syrup

> **TIP:** I love making this cake in a Bundt cake pan, but removing it is not so easy. These are my favorite tips for getting any cake out of a Bundt pan:
>
> Make sure you grease the Bundt pan well.
>
> Let your cake cool for about 15 minutes before trying to remove it. Before flipping it, with a dull knife, gently pull the cake away from the sides.
>
> When ready to flip the pan, put a plate on top of the pan and gently turn it over. With the dull knife, tap the outside of the pan on all sides to loosen the cake inside.
>
> Slowly lift the Bundt pan away from the cake. Don't fret if any cake sticks to the Bundt pan. Just sprinkle some powdered sugar over the cake, and you won't even see the imperfections!

CINNAMON-APPLE CRISP

(DF, EF, GF, NF, SF, V)

One simple fall pleasure: the cozy smell of baking apples. My oldest son gets all the credit for this dessert. After a wonderful autumn day of apple picking, he asked for a yummy apple dessert, inspiring the creation of this crisp. With just a handful of ingredients, you and your children can prepare this autumn delight. As it bakes, the tantalizing aroma will permeate every nook and cranny of your house. For extra-creamy indulgence, serve it with a scoop of your favorite vanilla ice cream. Should you be lucky enough to have leftovers, pair it with a maple latte for a grown-up breakfast treat.

Slicing apples provides a safe entryway for kids to start using knives in the kitchen. When teaching a new skill, model it slowly. Then, do the skill together side by side. Provide time for independent practice, but stay close and provide gentle correction until young novices gain confidence and safe, basic techniques. Don't err on the side of giving your child too dull of a knife. If it's not sharp enough to easily slice through an apple, your child can become frustrated, injured and develop bad habits.

Prep Time: 5 minutes   Cook Time: 25 minutes   Serves 8

Preheat the oven to 375°F (191°C). Coat a 9 x 13-inch (23 x 33-cm) baking dish with cooking spray.

In a medium bowl, stir together the oats, flour, brown sugar, oil and cinnamon.

Arrange the apples in an even layer in the prepared dish.

Sprinkle the oat mixture over the apples evenly.

Bake uncovered until the apples are tender and bubbling, and the topping is golden brown, about 25 minutes.

1 cup (90 g) old-fashioned oats, regular or gluten free

¾ cup (90 g) whole wheat or gluten-free flour

½ cup (110 g) firmly packed light brown sugar

½ cup (120 ml) avocado oil, melted coconut oil or vegetable oil

1 teaspoon ground cinnamon

6 Granny Smith apples, peeled or unpeeled, cut into 2-inch (5-cm) squares

> **TIPS:** Save time by not peeling the apples—that is what I do!
>
> You can always change up this recipe by using pears or peaches.

MIMA'S JELL-O RINGS

(DF, EF, GF, NF, SF, V)

This is one of those recipes that I know my boys will share with their children one day. It's a holiday family tradition that came from my stepmom, Mindy—aka Mima. This beloved recipe was passed down to Mima from her aunt Fanny. Three generations later, my boys love, love, love these yummy treats. Every holiday gathering, they know that Mima will be making them. They've been a constant in their lives, and they've affectionately renamed them "Mima's Jell-O Rings." No matter what else is on the holiday spread, they walk past it all, beelining to her dish.

You can choose your favorite flavor of Jell-O to use in this recipe, but heed this warning from Momma Chef: *Stay away from the reds!* We've learned the hard way that red Jell-O can stain holiday clothing and leave hideous stains on the carpet. Stick with any of these super delicious pairings with pineapple: yellow (lemon or Island Pineapple), orange or lime. With these flavors, if a ring slips out of your hand mid-gobble, you won't have to panic about cleanup. Your only worry will be to get your hands on another Jell-O Ring before they're all gone!

Prep Time: 5 minutes   Serves 6

Open one end of the pineapple ring can, and drain really well. (I drain it, let it sit for a few minutes, then drain it again.)

In a small mixing bowl, empty the packet of Jell-O, and mix in the hot water.

Pour the Jell-O into the pineapple can, and chill in the refrigerator for at least 2 hours, ideally overnight.

To unmold: Open the other end of the can, go around the edges with a thin knife, then ease out the loaf of Jell-O.

Slice through the Jell-O between the rings, and serve.

1 (20-ounce [567-g]) can sliced pineapple rings

1 (3-ounce [85-g]) package Jell-O, regular or vegan

1 cup (240 ml) hot water

SAVE ROOM FOR DESSERT

Growing up, my brother firmly believed (or at least, he wanted to convince our parents to believe) that the human stomach had two compartments—one for "regular" food and one specially designated for dessert. Too full to finish your peas, but more than able to fit in some after-dinner cookies? That's no problem with the dual-stomach theory. His argument was foolproof as to why dessert was always a good idea.

While thoughts of dessert should be as joyful as this memory, its enjoyment is sometimes marred by guilt. For whatever reason, indulging in a sweet treat sometimes feels wicked—or at least a bit naughty. However, Momma Chef has good news: desserts can be good for you! There's actual science and psychology that support having a healthy relationship with desserts. So, let us eat cake—or any of the scrumptious desserts in this chapter.

Vanilla-Baked Pears (page 213) will wow your family and guests with its simple elegance. There's something about plating it that makes me feel like I'm a chef at a four-star restaurant. Another sophisticated dessert is the Bourbon-Spiced Bread Pudding (page 218), an easy rendition of a New Orleans classic.

Hands down, the Chocolate Chip Cookie Pie (page 222) will be the hit of every slumber party and any Netflix-binge weekend. It also serves as a fun alternative to a traditional birthday cake.

Want to save a trip to your local donut shop and indulge in donuts right out of the oven? Try the Deliciously Easy Baked Chocolate Donuts (page 221). As an extra bonus, these donuts are baked, not fried.

My favorite pretty-as-a-picture dessert is the Strawberry Shortcake Trifle (page 229). Even people who don't post food pics on social media will be tempted to show off this beauty. They'll just have to be quick—this dessert doesn't last long!

I'm such a big believer in the power of desserts that my sweetest recipes could not be contained in just one chapter. Don't miss my other tasty recipes in the "What's In Your Kitchen" and "Cooking with Kids" chapters.

GOOEY S'MORES BROWNIES

(DF, NF, SF, V)

Some desserts belong to certain seasons: lemon sorbet sounds great in the summer, but in the dead of winter? Not so much. But what about those desserts that deserve year-round access? In honor of their favorite campfire treat, my boys created Gooey S'mores Brownies. Traditionally limited to fire pits in the summer, my family—and yours!—can now enjoy the taste of chocolate and melted marshmallows all year round. While baking, the marshmallows and chocolate chips melt into the brownies, creating an ooey, gooey, rich and chocolaty flashback to July nights around a fire.

Prep Time: 5 minutes   Cook Time: 20 minutes   Makes 12 brownies

Preheat the oven to 350°F (177°C). Coat a 9 x 13-inch (23 x 33-cm) baking dish with cooking spray.

In a large mixing bowl, add the brownie mix, ½ cup (30 g) of mini marshmallows, chocolate chips, oil, water and eggs, and mix by hand until well combined.

Pour the mixture into the prepared baking dish, then top with the 20 mini marshmallows, making sure they are evenly spread out over the mixture.

Bake uncovered on the lowest rack of your oven for 20 to 22 minutes until a toothpick comes out clean.

1 box (15- to 18-ounce [425- to 510-g]) chocolate brownie mix

½ cup (30 g) mini marshmallows, plus 20 extra mini marshmallows

⅓ cup (55 g) dairy-free chocolate chips

½ cup (120 ml) vegetable oil or melted coconut oil

⅓ cup (80 ml) water

2 eggs

> **TIPS:** If you are not making this recipe dairy free, you can use any chocolate chips that your kids prefer.
>
> This recipe is super easy to make gluten free. Just be sure to purchase a box of gluten-free brownie mix and follow the same instructions above.

NEW YORK–STYLE CHEESECAKE

(GF, NF, SF, V)

If you've ever been intimidated by making a cheesecake, join the club. This iconic dessert can strike fear into any cook's heart. No worries for you, though. This recipe will help you produce a deliciously creamy New York–style cheesecake that you'll be proud to claim as your own. You'll find that the addition of a little sour cream produces a texture as silky as Frank Sinatra's voice. Start spreading the news, for this cheesecake is pure New York, New York.

Today, most New Yorkers agree that a true slice of New York cheesecake is pure, unadulterated cheesecake. You don't have to be a purist, though: fruit (cherries!), crumbled cookies (Oreos!) or crushed candy (Heath bars!) make terrific toppings.

Prep Time: 5 minutes   Cook Time: 55 minutes   Serves 8

Preheat the oven to 350°F (177°C).

In a large mixing bowl, add the eggs and, using a hand mixer, blend on medium speed for 30 seconds.

Add the cream cheese, sugar, sour cream and vanilla to the eggs, and blend until smooth, about 3 minutes.

Pour the cheesecake mixture into the pie crust, and bake uncovered for 55 minutes until the center is firm.

Let the cheesecake cool in the refrigerator for at least 2 hours.

TIPS: You can use regular or low-fat cream cheese and sour cream in this recipe, but do not use the fat-free version.

You can make this recipe gluten free by using a gluten-free pie crust.

2 eggs

2 (8-ounce [232-g]) packages cream cheese, at room temperature

¾ cup (150 g) granulated sugar

½ cup (120 ml) sour cream

2 teaspoons (10 ml) vanilla extract

1 (9-inch [23-cm]) graham cracker pie crust (regular or gluten free)

VANILLA-BAKED PEARS

(DF, EF, GF, NF, SF, V)

To most kids—and many adults—the word "dessert" conjures up an ooey, gooey, sugary explosion. Expand their minds and serve this simple and truly delicious dessert to showcase the wholesome goodness of baked fruit. Baked pears are also one of those great last-minute dishes that you can easily pull together for unexpected company—and there's absolutely no need to share that this elegant dessert only took you 5 minutes to prepare. Like the apple crisp (see page 202), the fragrant aroma that fills your home will be more pleasing than the priciest scented candle on the market. Baked pears taste amazing alone, but I won't deny you a small scoop of vanilla ice cream or a dollop of whipped cream on the side.

BTW, these pears also make an out-of-this-world breakfast. Skip the ice cream and serve with Greek vanilla yogurt and some simple granola. Delicious!

Prep Time: 5 minutes   Cook Time: 40 minutes   Serves 8

Preheat the oven to 350°F (177°C).

Halve the pears, and scoop out the seeds.

Place the pears flesh side up in an 8 x 8-inch (20 x 20-cm) baking dish.

In a small bowl, mix the brown sugar, vanilla, orange juice and water, and pour this mixture evenly over the pears.

Bake the pears uncovered for 40 to 45 minutes until they are soft and lightly brown.

Place each pear with some of the liquid into an individual small bowl, and serve with vanilla ice cream.

4 large pears, any variety

¼ cup (55 g) light brown sugar

1 teaspoon vanilla extract

Juice of 1 small orange, about ¼ cup (60 ml)

¼ cup (60 ml) water

Vanilla ice cream, regular or dairy free, for serving

> **TIP:** You can use other fruit for this recipe as well. Try apples, peaches or apricots. Just make sure to remove the seeds or pits.

GRANDMA CINDY'S SNOWBALL COOKIES

(DF, EF, SF, V)

You've been tracing the common thread of my mom throughout this cookbook, right? (See pages 74, 86, 110 and 151.) Here's another Grandma Cindy special. I've been eating these cookies for as long as I can remember. I loved them growing up, and now my sons love them as well. Like the indulgent grandma she is, we don't need to ask her to make them—she just magically appears with a fresh batch! Odds are that my youngest son has a snack bag full of these cookies tucked away somewhere in his bedroom; he likes to have a few within arm's reach should the craving strike. I get it: These cookies are so addictive, I'm pretty sure I could eat an entire tray in one sitting. (Not to brag, but it's possible I have already achieved that goal. . . .)

Prep Time: 5 minutes   Cook Time: 15 minutes   Makes 3 dozen cookies

Preheat the oven to 325°F (163°C). Line a baking sheet with parchment paper.

In a large mixing bowl, add the butter, ½ cup (60 g) of the confectioners' sugar and the vanilla.

With a hand mixer on low speed, blend together for about 2 minutes. Then add in the flour and pecans, and blend on low for another 2 or 3 minutes until everything is well combined.

Shape the dough into 1-inch (2.5-cm) balls, and place them on the prepared baking sheet.

Bake uncovered for 15 minutes. Let the cookies cool completely.

Add the remaining ¼ cup (30 g) of confectioners' sugar to a zip-top bag. Place the cookie balls, about 5 at a time, carefully into the zip-top bag, and gently shake until they are completely coated in the confectioners' sugar.

1 cup (227 g) butter or margarine, softened

¾ cup (90 g) confectioners' sugar, divided

1 teaspoon vanilla extract

1½ cups (188 g) all-purpose flour

¾ cup (82 g) finely chopped pecans

> **TIPS:** Make sure to let these cookies cool completely before covering them in confectioners' sugar or the sugar will melt.
>
> If you are making this recipe dairy free, use margarine.

(EF, GF, NF, SF, V)

DECADENT CHOCOLATE FUDGE

Want to share some love? Use the universal currency of homemade fudge! You can make this mouthwatering confection and delight your friends, family, coworkers, neighbors, tutors, crossing guards and postal workers. Double the recipe and drop off a tray at the fire station or the teachers' lounge at your child's school. After cooling, wrap the fudge tightly in plastic wrap to keep it from drying out. For gifts, add some colorful cellophane and a festive ribbon. You could also include a copy of the recipe taped on top . . . or then again, maybe not. Let them think you spent more than 6 minutes stirring up this sweet gift!

Prep Time: 5 minutes   Serves 6

In a large microwave-safe bowl, combine the chocolate chips, butter and condensed milk. Microwave for 2 minutes.

Stir everything together, and microwave for another 90 seconds. Stir and repeat this step in 30-second increments until all the chocolate is melted.

Once the chocolate is fully melted, stir in the vanilla.

Coat a 9 x 9 x 2-inch (23 x 23 x 5-cm) pan with cooking spray, and pour the chocolate mixture evenly into the pan. Add any topping that you like, or you can make plain fudge.

Refrigerate for at least 1 hour until the fudge is set.

3 cups (504 g) semisweet chocolate chips

¼ cup (57 g) unsalted butter

1 (14-ounce [396-g]) can sweetened condensed milk

1 teaspoon vanilla extract

Toppings of choice (see Tip)

> TIP: Some topping suggestions are:
>
> **S'mores Fudge:** mini marshmallows and small graham cracker pieces
>
> **Salted Toffee:** chopped toffee bits and a dash of sea salt
>
> **Candy Cane:** chopped candy canes (my favorite!)
>
> The possibilities are endless. Have your kids join in on the fun by adding their favorite toppings.

BOURBON-SPICED BREAD PUDDING

(NF, SF, V)

I grew up with much of my extended family living out of state. Imagine my *delight* when one of my closest cousins, Amy, married a Chicago man and transplanted here from New York. Imagine my *joy* when Amy started working with me at the same nonprofit organization. Imagine my *ecstasy* when Amy brought this bourbon bread pudding to our work potluck (the very same potluck where the kugel recipe on page 85 debuted). I was obsessed after the first bite. Amy's recipe originated with her aunt from the "other side," so I was thrilled to introduce it to our side of the family. I've been making and tweaking it for 20 years and counting.

Fortunately/unfortunately, most of the alcohol in the bourbon cooks off, making it safe for my kids to eat.

Prep Time: 5 minutes   Cook Time: 45 minutes   Serves 8

Coat a 9 x 13-inch (23 x 33-cm) baking dish with cooking spray, and add the brioche cubes to the dish.

In a medium bowl, using a hand mixer on medium speed, blend the milk, eggs, brown sugar, bourbon and pumpkin pie spice for about 3 minutes.

Pour the milk mixture evenly over the bread.

Cover the baking dish with foil or plastic wrap, and let it sit in the refrigerator for about 1 hour so the bread can absorb all the other ingredients.

When you're ready to bake, preheat the oven to 350°F (177°C). Bake the bread pudding uncovered for 40 to 45 minutes, or until a toothpick comes out clean.

Remove from the oven, and let it sit for 5 to 10 minutes before serving.

6 cups (240 g) cubed brioche bread (see Tips)

3 cups (720 ml) whole or 2 percent milk

4 eggs, beaten

½ cup (110 g) packed light brown sugar

2 tablespoons (30 ml) bourbon

1 teaspoon pumpkin pie spice

TIPS: I keep pumpkin pie spice in my pantry. I like to use it in many fall recipes. You can find it at most grocery stores. If you don't have it on hand, you can use 1 teaspoon ground cinnamon and a small dash of ground nutmeg.

You can substitute soft challah bread for the brioche.

DELICIOUSLY EASY BAKED CHOCOLATE DONUTS

(NF, SF, V)

If you grew up in a certain era, you're familiar with the commercial slogan: "It's time to make the donuts!" Fast forward 30 years, and my sons have fully adopted that philosophy: *Anytime* is a good time to make the donuts. Their love of fried dough inspired me to make a delicious baked version. Plus, it's simple enough that anyone can "make the donuts!" All you need are four ingredients, a donut pan and 5 minutes of prep! I hear you thinking, "A donut pan, Karen? Really?" Yes. A donut pan. I'm not a huge believer in one-trick-pony kitchen tools, but this purchase is worth it. You're going to want to get one delivered ASAP.

Prep Time: 5 minutes   Cook Time: 12 minutes   Makes 15 to 18 donuts

Preheat the oven to 350°F (177°C). Lightly coat two donut pans with nonstick cooking spray.

In a large bowl, combine the cake mix, milk, oil and eggs. Mix well.

Fill each donut cup three-quarters full.

Bake uncovered for 11 to 14 minutes, or until a toothpick comes out clean.

Let the donuts cool for 5 to 10 minutes before removing them from the donut pan.

1 (15.25-ounce [432-g]) box devil's food cake mix

¾ cup (180 ml) 2 percent or whole milk

¼ cup (60 ml) avocado or vegetable oil

2 eggs, beaten

> **TIPS:** You can top these donuts with your favorite frosting and sprinkles. Just wait for the donuts to cool before decorating.
>
> An easy glaze to add to these donuts can be made by mixing 1 cup (120 g) of confectioners' sugar and 2 tablespoons (30 ml) of milk or water. You can then dip the donuts in the glaze, and let the glaze harden for about 5 minutes.

CHOCOLATE-CHIP COOKIE PIE

(DF, NF, SF, V)

One Saturday afternoon, I found myself with a house full of hungry kids hankering for a sweet treat. I knew that freshly baked chocolate-chip cookies would be a crowd-pleaser, but, ugh. I didn't want to scoop, drop, bake and cool batches of cookies all afternoon. Light bulb! *Cookie Pie*! It literally (and I mean *literally*) took me less than 5 minutes to get this crowd-pleasing concoction in the oven. The smell of homemade goodness spread through the house and by the time the oven timer buzzed, I had a group of eager taste testers ready for a warm slice of cookie pie. Not one crumb remained 30 minutes later! Adding a handful of chopped pecans to the mixture before baking is a divine variation. A favorite modification for kids is to reduce the chocolate chips to ½ cup (42 g) and add ½ cup (42 g) of M&M's.

Prep Time: 5 minutes   Cook Time: 25 minutes   Serves 6

Preheat the oven to 350°F (177°C). Coat a 9½-inch (24-cm) pie dish with cooking spray.

In a large mixing bowl, add the eggs and, using a hand mixer on high speed, beat the eggs for 1 minute or until foamy.

Add the flour, brown sugar, vanilla and butter, and mix on medium speed for another 2 minutes, until everything is well combined.

Then with a spoon, stir in the chocolate chips.

Pour the mixture evenly into the pie dish.

Bake uncovered for 25 minutes, or until a toothpick comes out clean.

2 eggs

1 cup (125 g) all-purpose flour

¾ cup (165 g) packed light brown sugar

1 teaspoon vanilla extract

½ cup (1 stick; 114 g) butter, softened, or ½ cup (120 ml) melted coconut oil

1 cup (168 g) semisweet or dark chocolate chips

TIPS: If you are making this recipe dairy free, make sure to use melted coconut oil and dairy-free chocolate chips.

You can also make these as chocolate-chip cupcakes. Just grease a muffin pan and fill each well three-quarters full with batter. The baking time will decrease to 15 to 18 minutes, or until a toothpick comes out clean.

MERINGUE COOKIES WITH BERRIES

(DF, GF, NF, SF, V)

Airy, delicate and lovely meringue cookies simply make me happy. I'm not surprised that Marie Antoinette loved them; meringues look like a dreamy treat made for royalty. Slightly crunchy on the outside and creamy on the inside, these little clouds of wonder also rule as they are low in calories and fat. A guilt-free delight. These cookies look fancy, but they're actually quite simple to make. My favorite part is watching the egg whites fluff up into glossy white peaks. Get your crown ready, because you'll be the queen (or king) of the kitchen when you serve up these marvelous meringue cookies!

Prep Time: 5 minutes   Cook Time: 45 minutes   Makes 20 to 25 cookies

Preheat the oven to 225°F (107°C). Line two baking sheets with parchment paper.

In a large mixing bowl, combine the egg whites and cream of tartar.

Using a hand mixer on medium speed, whip the egg whites until small peaks form.

Gradually add in the sugar, and keep whipping the mixture until stiff peaks form; it should now be a bit glossy. Stiff peaks happen when you lift the mixer, and the peaks lift up and do not fall down.

With a spoon, gently fold in the vanilla.

Using a spoon, drop 2-inch (5-cm) circles on the prepared baking sheets, making sure there is a little room between the cookies.

Bake the meringue cookies uncovered for 45 minutes.

Turn off the oven, open the oven door and let the meringue cookies sit in the oven for another 30 minutes.

I like to serve these with fresh berries on top or on the side of the cookies.

5 egg whites, at room temperature

½ teaspoon cream of tartar

1¼ cups (225 g) granulated sugar

½ teaspoon vanilla extract

1 cup (120 to 150 g) fresh berries, optional

> **TIP:** The egg whites *cannot* have any of the yolks in them. So, what I like to do is break each egg into a separate small bowl, and then put them in the large mixing bowl. That way, if any yolk gets into the small bowl, you can just toss out that one egg white.

MAPLE BUNDT CAKE

(NF, SF, V)

I'm not ashamed to say that I jump on the pumpkin-spice train every September. However, my heart of hearts belongs to maple, the classic of classic fall flavors. My favorite way to enjoy the warm flavor of maple is in baked goods, especially this Bundt cake. You'll want to share a slice with a friend over coffee or add it to a brunch menu. BTW, maple syrup does *not* equal pancake syrup. Check the label to ensure that the syrup you're using is 100 percent maple syrup and not merely "maple flavored." It makes a difference, but don't be intimidated by the range of pure-syrup prices; paying more does not necessarily mean a better product. Try what's on sale, and experiment to find what you like. In brief, the darker the color, the stronger the maple flavor.

Prep Time: 5 minutes   Cook Time: 35 minutes   Serves 8

Preheat the oven to 350°F (177°C). Coat a 10-inch (25-cm) Bundt pan with cooking spray.

In a large mixing bowl, add the flour, sour cream, oil, sugar and eggs. Using a hand mixer on medium speed, blend all the ingredients together until well combined.

Pour the batter into the prepared Bundt pan.

Bake uncovered for about 35 minutes, or until a toothpick inserted into the center of the cake comes out clean.

Allow the cake to cool for at least 15 minutes, and remove it from the Bundt cake pan.

Pour the maple syrup over the cake.

1¼ cup (156 g) self-rising flour

1 (8-ounce [240-ml]) container sour cream

½ cup (120 ml) vegetable oil

1¼ cups (150 g) granulated sugar

3 eggs

¼ cup (60 ml) pure maple syrup

> **TIPS:** See my tips on page 201 for the best way to remove a cake from a Bundt pan.
>
> You can also bake this in a greased 9 x 13-inch (23 x 33-cm) pan. If you do this, you can pour the maple syrup right over the cake while it's in the pan.

STRAWBERRY SHORTCAKE TRIFLE

(NF, SF, V)

Here in the Windy City, I'm only 25 miles away from the Art Institute of Chicago, home of Monet's *Water Lilies*, a jaw-dropping Seurat and the iconic *American Gothic*—that stoic farming couple with a pitchfork. Whether or not you enjoy looking at art, you'll love making—and eating—this visually stunning trifle. While it would taste delicious in any serving dish, the whole point of a trifle is to create some eye candy to dazzle the dessert table. If you don't have a trifle dish, you can look for one, as my friend did, at a thrift store. Older relatives often have a trifle serving dish to lend. In a pinch, you could make a deep glass bowl work. When dishing out your showstopper dessert, use a large serving spoon so you can vertically pull out every delicious layer.

Prep Time: 6 minutes   Serves 6 to 8

Make the whipped cream. In a large mixing bowl, add the heavy cream and sugar. Using a hand mixer on medium speed, whip the cream and sugar until medium peaks form, about 4 minutes.

Layer the trifle. Start with one-third of the pound cake squares on the bottom of the dish, then spread one-third of the pudding on the cake. Lay one-third of the bananas on the pudding. Next spread one-third of the whipped cream over the bananas. Lay one-third of the sliced strawberries on the whipped cream. Repeat these steps until you have three layers, with the strawberries finishing off the trifle.

1 (16-ounce [480-ml]) container heavy cream, cold

¼ cup granulated sugar (50 g) or confectioners' sugar (30 g)

1 (16-ounce [454-g]) pound cake, sliced into 1-inch (2.5-cm) squares

1 cup (240 ml) premade vanilla pudding

2 bananas, peeled and sliced, optional

2 pounds (907 g) strawberries, stems removed and berries cut in half

TIPS: This recipe can easily be made gluten free by using a gluten-free pound cake or sponge cake.

I love bananas in my trifle, but if you prefer without, you can leave them out.

If you're more of a chocolate fiend, replace the pound cake with brownie bites, the vanilla pudding with chocolate, use your favorite fruit (raspberries are a great choice!), and shave some chocolate curls on top.

MOMMA CHEF'S SOUP KITCHEN AND LITTLE FREE PANTRIES

Of all the recipes in this book, here is the most important. It's a recipe for life, and—yes!—it has fewer than six ingredients! It's taken from Ralph Waldo Emerson: "The purpose of life is not to be happy. It is to be useful, to be honorable, to be compassionate, to have it make some difference that you have lived and lived well." Below are a couple of ways that I've been putting my own spin on Emerson's recipe.

In June 2018, my life was full, and I was happy. My cooking blog, Momma Chef, was blowing up. I was busy writing articles for dozens of magazines and working with multiple companies to develop recipes for their products. My family—as always—kept my days exciting. It was like a dream come true . . . yet I did not feel complete. Something was off. What was it?

Amidst my endeavors and engagements, my brain must have been secretly percolating on finding an answer. My "aha" moment arrived at 3 a.m. when I woke up with a big idea. I had found my missing ingredient: My table wasn't big enough! Yes, my dining room table could sit 12 while my blogging "table" had thousands of cyber-seats. My early morning vision was to extend my table to feed the hungry by opening a soup kitchen—a safe, clean and uplifting environment to service underprivileged and under-resourced families.

Once the idea came to me, I was determined to make it happen. Over the next few months, I threw myself into research and networking. I created a business plan, held fundraisers to offset costs and designed menus to feed more than 100 people. A wonderful facility agreed to donate its space. Within four months—in October 2018—Momma Chef's Soup Kitchen opened its doors at Congregation K.I.N.S. in Chicago.

Every week Momma Chef's Soup Kitchen provides a hot, homemade, five-course meal to anyone who comes to our doors, and we also deliver 70 meals to two shelters in Chicago. We all volunteer our time, using more than 600 volunteers per year to prepare and serve meals. My June 2018 middle-of-the-night epiphany has now provided more than 20,000 meals and counting since we first opened our doors.

On some level, I must always be thinking about food because about 2 years later, inspiration struck again! I happened upon a Little Free Library—you've probably seen them in a neighborhood, park or parking lot. They're cute homemade wooden boxes, housing free books for anyone to take home. It struck me that I could use this same notion to address food insecurity around Chicago. That day, I pledged to myself to start the Momma Chef Little Free Pantry movement to provide 24-hour access to nonperishable food for anyone in need.

mommachef's
SOUP KITCHEN

HELP US CHANGE THE WORLD- ONE MEAL AT A TIME!

LITTLE FREE PANTRY

BROUGHT TO YOU BY
Momma Chef's Soup Kitchen

If you do the math, you'll realize that particular moment of inspiration took place just as COVID-19 was creating a "new normal." The pandemic outbreak and subsequent shutdown made this idea more difficult to complete, yet more urgent than ever. In May 2021, the first pantry opened and two more followed. We keep the pantries stocked daily with healthy, nonperishable food. It's a wonderful way for people in need to take food anonymously at any time of the day.

Let me encourage you to listen to that voice that wakes you up at 3 a.m. with a dream to make the world a better place. I believe in you!

A huge thank you for purchasing this cookbook! A portion of its proceeds will be donated to Momma Chef's Soup Kitchen and Little Free Pantries. Together we are changing the world—one meal at a time.

ABOUT THE AUTHOR

KAREN NOCHIMOWSKI, the mom behind the popular food blog Momma Chef, has loved cooking for as long as she can remember. After friends and family begged to be let in on her culinary secrets, she created a blog featuring easy and quick recipes that everyone loved. Karen wants to help busy people serve fabulous family meals with less effort. All her recipes are made using fewer than six ingredients and no more than 6 minutes of prep time.

Through the popularity of the Momma Chef blog, Karen and her recipes have been featured in dozens of magazines and online publications, including *HuffPost*, *Working Mother*, *Costco Connection*, *TODAY Parents*, *Chicago Parent* and the *Chicago Tribune*, among others. She's been a featured speaker at MommyCon, WGN radio and *LIVE with Kelly and Ryan*. Currently, she's the monthly food columnist for the *Daily Herald*.

A vast cyber community fell in love not only with Karen's recipes, but also with her genuine warmth and humor. She doesn't pretend to be the perfect mom with an idealized Instagram-worthy life. She finds joy in the natural chaos of raising three boys, and she isn't afraid to share the relatable hilarity that provides the backstories behind many of her picture-perfect recipes. Just ask her about what she's willing to sacrifice in order to make the perfect salmon. Here's a clue: it involves a basement carpet and a creative 3-year-old during his toilet-training days.

When she's not wrangling her sons, dreaming of tropical travels or chasing her dog, Karen loves to host dinner parties for her family and friends. Her love language? Food. Motivated to spread this love beyond her own kitchen table, she founded Momma Chef's Soup Kitchen on the north side of Chicago in 2018. Three years later, she pioneered the Momma Chef Little Free Pantry movement, 24/7 outdoor pantries stocked with nonperishable food for those in need.

Karen lives in the Chicagoland area with her husband, three active sons and her baby "girl," aka Gingee the Labradoodle. Should you find yourself in her neighborhood, you can't miss her. She'll be the one inviting you over for coffee and a bite of banana bread, fresh from the oven.

ACKNOWLEDGMENTS

When it comes to giving shout-outs, you can kiss goodbye to Momma Chef's "six ingredients, six-minute prep" rule. Carve out some time, readers: My list of thanks is as full as my grateful heart.

Thank you to my three amazing boys. Every single day, you put a smile on my face and love in my heart. We may have a very loud and active house, but I wouldn't change a thing. You three have given me the most important job and title I will ever carry—*Mom*.

Thank you to my husband, my true soul mate. Izzy, you believe in my dreams and make me believe I can do anything. I love that you love every meal I make for you. I could not have done any of this without your unwavering support, and I can't imagine being on this wonderful journey with anyone but you.

Thank you, Mom. You're the best possible role model a girl can have. Thank you for teaching me the power of a home-cooked meal. You have been my boys' second mom, and they are beyond lucky to have you.

Thank you, Mindy, for the countless hours you spent helping get my blog off the ground. Somehow, when I can't think of a creative way to write something, you are always there to give me the best advice.

Thank you to Marissa at Page Street Publishing; I am so humbled and grateful that you took a chance on me! Your guidance and ideas have brought this cookbook to life. To Meg and Katie: Thank you for seeing my vision and beautifully presenting it on these pages. I am so fortunate to be working with all of you at Page Street.

Thank you, Kristine—my editor and my biggest cheerleader. You have been with me from day one. You have pushed me, challenged me and helped me get my words on paper. I could not have done any of this without you. And thanks to your girls for trying out the recipes in this cookbook and the awesome tips.

Thank you to Yvette for your countless, countless hours designing everything from my logos, proposal, soup kitchen flyers, posters and so much more. You are so beyond talented!

(continued)

ACKNOWLEDGMENTS (CONTINUED)

Thanks to Jen and everyone at Bradford Literary for helping to make this cookbook deal happen. Jen, you had me at, "I made the honey-curry chicken and it's *amazing*."

Thank you, Shana and Elan, for letting me pass probably every dish in this book over the fence and being the best taste testers. And Shana, thank you for encouraging me to write this cookbook and for the hours upon hours you spent during the past year listening to every detail of this book.

Thank you to Karen E. for agreeing all those years ago to be my volunteer coordinator for the soup kitchen; there is no way I would have made it this far without you by my side.

Thank you to my amazing friends and family. You have always been there for me with your unwavering support and spot-on advice. You keep me sane and grounded, and you love my boys like they are your own. It takes a village, and I love that you are mine.

Thank you to all my loyal Momma Chef followers and readers of this cookbook. Your comments, feedback, suggestions, photos and praise motivate me to keep moving forward. In 2018, when a follower wrote to me, "Thank you, Karen, for the first time I felt like a real hero in the kitchen," I knew this was my path.

INDEX

3 1170 01189 2167